A Moose In The Distance
And Other Thoughts On
Organizational Performance

By Jeffrey M. Saltzman

Published by Kenexa®
Corporate Headquarters:
650 East Swedesford Road, Second Floor
Wayne, PA 19087
© 2007 Kenexa
All rights reserved.
ISBN 978-0-9800252-0-0
Edited by: Stephanie Sparks
Creative Direction: Andrea L. Watkins
Illustrations: Deb Lee
www.kenexa.com

Table of Contents

INTRODUCTION

~

FROM THE AUTHOR

In December 2006, I was approached by my new company and asked if I would start writing a blog. Not really knowing what this would entail, but in the spirit of a willingness to try new things, I signed on. I was unsure what form or what topics the blog should take. Kenexa, in its generous spirit, posed no limitations, no overarching theme and no restrictions on what I could write about. I thought long and hard about the format and topics that I could knowledgeably speak about. I have to admit to a lot of uncertainty; I have never thought of myself as much of a writer, even though ideas for topic areas flashed through my head.

I first thought I should write short pieces about the methods used to conduct organizational surveys. After all, I had been conducting and overseeing organizational surveys for more than 20 years. Surely, I must have something to say about that. But slowly, as I started to put pen to paper (key strokes to computer screen actually, but pen to paper sounds better), what naturally flowed out was observations about the world of work and the world in which we live from the perspective of employees living within it. The pieces I wrote were meant to stimulate thought and do not contain all the answers organizationally—although I have to admit to a certain bias regarding the way things should be done that comes through clearly in my writing.

While the pieces that I wrote are not scientific papers and are based simply on my observations, most of my observing over the years has been data based. My observations come from looking at how millions and millions of employees from all over the world have responded to organizational surveys—surveys that cumulatively have covered a wide range of topics and face-to-face interviews with thousands of employees that have provided additional insight about the companies in which they work. I consider a posting well written if after reading one you can see aspects of yourself or your company in the work.

For the last year, I have been writing commentary and posting it about once a week, sometimes twice a week. Because my blog has been fairly popular, Kenexa approached me again and asked me to pick out my favorite pieces for publication. Again, I was a little apprehensive because a publication is different than a short blog posting that is knocked out over a weekend.

Picking out my favorites was tough, and so to some extent, I let the popularity of the pieces—the most requested—guide me. Therefore, this book contains my favorite and your favorite blog pieces posted since December 2006, which I also think are most relevant to the world of work. They are organized in a fashion that hopefully makes sense from a reader's point of view and are not necessarily in chronological order. There has been some editing to clean up my grammar, punctuation and some awkward or unclear phrases, but in essence these pieces are as they first appeared as blog postings. A big thank you goes to Stephanie Sparks for undertaking that editing task.

I hope you enjoy the pieces.
Jeffrey Saltzman

THERE IS SOMETHING FISHY ABOUT EMPLOYEE SELECTION

THURSDAY, DECEMBER 14, 2006

TALENT

Predictably, analogs exist between the natural world and the organizational world. Lessons drawn from nature, when applied correctly, potentially hold great benefits for organizations. One has only to determine how these natural patterns are shared by humans or exist within our "human" environment. For example, one that immediately springs to mind includes the Intentional Stance, an animal's innate tendency and survival aid to ascribe deliberate intent to movement, rustling noises or other sounds—even though those sounds may be no more than the wind or other random event. Or there's the development of superstitious behavior in animals, displaying repetitious but inconsequential behavior patterns they—and humans—believe will help find food or shelter or a mate (or in the case of baseball players, get a hit or score a run), or the science of chaos that can mathematically describe the shape of a leaf and movements within the stock market.

Sometimes, the techniques that humans develop to help their own decision making process can be used to describe patterns in nature. Take for instance critical mass decision making, which has been around since WWII. It is a method used to tap into the knowledge that exists within large groups of people and extract useful information. It has been used for tasks as diverse as finding sunken submarines, predicting elections and determining terrorist targets. I believe that it holds great potential for organizations to tap into the natural intelligence already located within their firms. I am waiting for a biologist to discover that the patterns exhibited by groups of animals, from herds of zebra to flocks of birds, demonstrate critical mass decision making—this hidden group intelligence—to increase their chances of survival.

Then there are fish. What do fish know about employee selection? Well, it turns out, to be quite a bit. I hope you enjoy this short piece and it leaves you with at least a shadow of a smile.

~ ~ ~

Fish know a thing or two about employee selection—coral reef fish, specifically. They employ a very interesting method to determine whom they should hire while interviewing candidates for a job.

Coral reef fish experience what must be an uncomfortable sensation. Parasites attach themselves to the skin of coral reef fish. In order to rid themselves of the parasites, these fish visit and employ "cleaner" fish that remove the parasites. How do coral reef fish know which cleaner fish will be best for parasite removal? They have developed employee (fish) selection skills—skills that are useful for human managers to understand as they look at potential job candidates.

The cleaner fish have a choice as they work on grooming the coral reef fish. They can work diligently eating parasites off the coral reef fish, or they can chomp on what has been described as a delicious bite of mucous membrane (I assume it hurts to have a cleaner fish bite your mucus membrane) to get a more tasty meal than just parasites. It has been shown that when other coral reef fish are nearby watching, the cleaner fish are more likely to behave appropriately—foregoing nibbles on mucus membranes. This gives you a sense of what appropriate supervision can do, but it also demonstrates that the cleaner fish know what is expected of them on the job. I wonder who wrote that job description.

It gets really interesting when coral reef fish that have witnessed the desired behavior from the cleaner fish. They are more likely to choose, for their own cleaning, those fish behaving in the desired fashion. The coral reef fish are in essence interviewing candidates for the position by observing the cleaners' on-the-job performance and selecting the fish that performs best. They seem to instinctively know that one of the best predictors of future behavior is past behavior. I had to go to graduate school to learn this, so I wonder what that says about me.

What can we learn from this about employee selection? Human behavior often has parallels in other animals. When psychologists study personality characteristics, they have found it becomes very difficult for people to change as they age. Around 30 years of age, personality traits seem locked-in. One theory of personality describes how people can change if they undergo an "unfreeze–change–refreeze" experience. Yet the "unfreeze" events—events that have the potential to "unlock" personality characteristics or behaviors—tend to be of a fairly significant nature for the person. The point is that people lean toward consistency in the experiences they seek out and in how they behave. One of the best indicators of how an employee will perform on the job is past job performance. Don't expect an immature 40-year old manager who acts immaturely to suddenly find a mature side, or anticipate someone who exhibits marginal ethics to suddenly walk the straight and narrow or hope that an employee who is generally sloppy or last minute in his or her work to suddenly become fastidious and timely—at least not without a very significant event to propel them. Even then, the rates of recidivism will be extraordinarily high.

The goal of psychologists when they construct assessment centers or develop job-based testing for selection is the same as the coral reef fish. That is, to set up a situation where on-the-job behaviors can be observed in order to get a sense as to how the candidate will perform in the future. In the case of the psychologist, it's from a simulated or historical standpoint, and in the case of the fish, it's by direct observation. The use of biodata, such as job history, promotions, credit worthiness or even speeding tickets, is another method to examine past behavior.

Selecting the right employee for the job—an individual who fits correctly into the organization and has the necessary skill set—is absolutely critical. Do not take the coral reef fish example and the tendency of people to behave consistently to mean that there is no benefit in developing or training employees. In fact, just the opposite is true. Employees can benefit tremendously from having someone "show them the ropes" of how to be high performers in the organization. They may have the correct personality or skill set, but they may lack experience or some other component that would allow them to excel. Development of these people can be very advantageous—especially early in their careers. However, if you have an experienced employee or manager who consistently exhibits behaviors that are not appropriate (biting mucous membranes for instance), don't keep holding out hope that they will someday change their behavior if just given one more chance. It may be a fool's vigil.

SLACK

TUESDAY, DECEMBER 12, 2006

PERFORMANCE

There is enormous pressure for conformity within our society. Are you reading the right books? Driving the right car? Do your children go to the right schools? Conforming to societal norms confers status. It makes you seem to be like others who are deemed successful—others you want to be like. Authors buy up copies of their books in order to spur demand. For example, in 1995, the authors of a management book bought 50,000 copies of their own book from stores that *The New York Times* monitored in order to land on the best sellers list, which it did. The book then continued to do well despite mediocre reviews. Restaurants routinely fill the seats by the windows so passersby can see that others have selected to eat at the restaurant. Advertisements for clothes, cars, food and other products show attractive, successful people using the product, inferring that if you use the product, you too can be like these people.

We, of course, are no different from our cousins in the natural world. Researchers at the Yerkes Primate Center recently reported that apes conform to cultural norms. In this case, they performed a task the same way that other apes in the group did, even if an alternative method was available. They wanted to fit in, to be like the others.

What was not discussed, and would be a fascinating next step, is to determine the course of action the apes would take if it were obvious that the alternative method was clearly superior to the commonly used method. Would this confer status on the "innovator," or would he or she be pushed to the side with lowered status?

Not surprisingly, the desire to conform and the pressures to conform extend to the business environment as well. Organizations create rules to deal with the five to 10 percent of the population who do not conform to their standards. The tendency is to push people to the middle of the distribution, toward behaving like others in the group. This can create a "keep your head down" kind of mentality, with mediocrity as its chief beneficiary in the organization. (Some organizations pride themselves on being nontraditional innovative, non-conforming organizations. These organizations may have set up a culture that pushes "conforming to our non-conformity," which is a topic worthy of a separate piece). Organizations clearly have to manage their resources in order to achieve their goals, but is anything suffering in the commonly used practices that have developed?

I want to turn to the world of quality control—Six Sigma—for a possible answer. Within the world of Six Sigma, there is a paradox that is articulated as follows: to attain Six Sigma performance, we must minimize process variability (make our processes and outcomes conform), as well as minimizing slack and redundancy by building variability, slack and redundancy into our organizations. In other words, in order to constantly improve performance, room must be made in the organization for investigation, the vetting of alternative methods and procedures.

Wait a minute. Today's organizations are lean and mean. You have to constantly do more with less. Organizations have downsized, resulting in fewer people, but the amount of work required does not often adjust. You can't be efficient and get all this work done if you build in extra resources to test new procedures and methods. But you must.

Long-term process improvement and organizational success depend on it.

With the goal of improving organizational performance in mind, the path does not begin with stamping out all variability to make everything conform to a certain standard. Variability needs to be understood through rigorous measurement; it needs to be controlled in order to minimize defects or errors, but removing all variability eliminates the ability of the organization to learn from itself, and eliminates opportunities to improve. Variability is needed in order for improvement to occur.

Here is an example to illustrate that point. If you are examining 200 departments within an organization and there is no variation what-soever, you cannot learn much. You cannot conclude from the 15 departments that do "A," that "A" leads to more positive outcomes, such as lower levels of employee turnover, compared to the 15 departments that do "B." In this case "A" and "B" can be the same thing, but at different levels. For example, "A" might be a high level of employee engagement, whereas "B" might be a low level of engagement. By examining these differences, the organization can learn that it can improve. Without variation, you cannot learn; you cannot determine that "A" leads to one outcome and "B" to another.

In addition to variability, include the concept of redundancy. Redundancy is needed in order to allow for experimentation. Redundancy is when two different approaches are available to achieve a desired outcome. For instance, redundancy occurs when using a stamping machine to form a part from sheet metal or using powdered metal to form the same part in a mold under pressure. Which procedure is better and leads to lower costs, less waste, fewer defects and better part performance?

By being able to breathe through the nose and mouth, a redundancy, nature could experiment with noses for other potential uses—as in the elephant's trunk. If the elephant could not breathe through its mouth, it would be in a precarious position if it filled its trunk with water and then needed a breath.

By having people perform a task using more than one method, it is possible to determine if any method is more advantageous than another is. Upon standardizing around the more advantageous method, one immediately begins investigating other methods to see if those new methods yield even more improvement. This requires slack, the controlled embrace of variability and redundancy.

Through work I have done over the years, it appears that organizations with strong diversity programs outperform similar organizations without such programs. Having people with different backgrounds and skill sets from different cultures sets the stage for the organization to potentially have knowledge of the variety of processes and procedures available and to have within the organization different points of view. This assumes that these different points of view are valued and those with them are not ostracized. It is another way to embrace variability and for an organization to learn from itself.

At the Max Planck Institute, it was recently demonstrated that apes possess a surprising understanding of tools and even make plans to use them. In one experiment, an ape that came into a room, bringing with it the wrong tool to complete a task (it could not go back to get the correct tool), was able to shape the existing tool into a new tool to successfully complete the task. I don't know about you, but I am proud of my cousins, and I wonder if we can learn to shape new and improved business tools out of the ones we currently use.

ERRORS

SATURDAY, JULY 21, 2007

PERFORMANCE

*"If you pick up a starving dog and make him prosperous, he will not bite you.
This is the principal difference between a dog and a man."*
—Mark Twain

We all make errors. They're part of life. I have made more than a few, and some of them were big ones. When an error occurs by an employee inside an organization, the employee may be concerned that the overriding motivation on the part of management is not simply to learn from the error and put into place corrective actions, but to take retribution against the employee. This can often be the case no matter what the organization says regarding its motivation to find the cause of the errors and to learn from mistakes so that they don't reoccur.

One clue that brings you to this conclusion is seen in emails informing everyone that an error has been discovered in which the identity of the person who committed the error is kept secret. This is a sure sign that not everyone is operating with, or has everyone else convinced, that the organization is operating with, a no retribution, "let's learn from our mistakes" kind of philosophy.

It seems like some organizations are constantly trying to learn from the same kind of mistakes over and over again. It is like having one year of experience 20 times. One approach that can get organizations out of this rut is to employ an organizing framework. An organizing framework allows errors to be examined systematically within that framework, and for conclusions to be drawn regarding what needs to change to prevent the error from occurring once again. It is like the old joke, "How many psychologists does it take to change a light bulb? Only one, but the light bulb has to really want to change." Organizations, when they examine and properly conclude the causes of their errors, still have to really want to change. Knowledge of the cause does not fix the problem.

First, there is the issue of whether the employees are capable of doing the job from a basic knowledge, skills and ability standpoint. This issue is a selection issue, and for our immediate purposes, let's put that aside and assume that the people who have been put into the job, if the conditions were right, could actually perform it. With the framework that I use, there are just a few questions that help get at the heart of the matter.

First question: *Do the employees know how to do a good job?*

A failing grade on this first question could be due to issues of messaging within the organization or perhaps performance. From a messaging standpoint, has it been made clear what the definition is of a good job? Do the employees know what criteria levels are defined as good or error free? From a performance perspective, have employees been given the training they need so that they know how to perform in an error-free fashion?

Second question: *Do the employees have the resources needed to do a good job?*

The best messaging is for naught if employees don't have the resources they need to perform error free.

Resources can be thought of very broadly in three main categories.
1. Information
2. Physical Environment
3. Processes

Information includes knowledge about how to do the job, including relevant training. It also includes information flows that enable a job to be performed correctly. For instance, a production report is an information flow that allows an employee to predict accurately when an item might be shipped.

Physical Environment includes the needed equipment, staffing levels, organizational structure, etc. If one person is put in a three-person job, you can be sure he or she will have problems. Or if one person is simply not given the appropriate amount of time to do a good job, he or she will have trouble. Likewise, if the necessary computer equipment or other equipment is not provided, it is difficult to get the job done. Remember the old adage, "the right tool for the right job."

Processes cover administrative issues, engineering and science. Administratively for instance, can a bill be sent out correctly and within an acceptable period? When a customer calls, can they get through to someone who can help them? From an engineering perspective, do the business and manufacturing or service processes ones that make sense? Do they optimize resources? Is the appropriate person, with the appropriate skill set and background doing the appropriate job? Does the workflow make sense? Are unnecessary processes eliminated? From a science standpoint, are the basic business products or processes based on sound science? For instance, if you are in the oil industry, but you can't get the geology right and keep digging in the wrong spot, the rest doesn't matter.

Third question: *Do the employees care enough to do a good job?*

The appropriate information and resources may be in place, but if the individual employee does not care, or is rewarded for the wrong behavior, then it is again unlikely that the desired outcome will be achieved. We all know that you get what you reward, so examine what you are rewarding. If you are rewarding X, don't expect A.

The other aspect of just not caring is potentially one of the most complex. It involves the entire culture that the organization has set up, which is why this can give the company an unbeatable edge. Processes and products can be reverse engineered; prices can be even more easily matched. Yet duplicating a culture and the resultant ways individuals within a culture interact with customers and care about their work can be very difficult to match to a successful competitor.

It involves the whole gestalt of how the organization is viewed by the employee. Is the place effectively managed? Does the organization really care about its people? Do people get a fair shake here? At the individual level, what is in it for me? Why should I stick around this place? And do people have a sense of future that if they stick around, good things can happen for them?

When errors occur, working through these questions systematically can help the organization determine the correct course of action so the organization can implement lasting improvement, thereby reducing its number of errors and learning from its history.

> *"An error doesn't become a mistake until you refuse to correct it."*
> *-Orlando A. Battista*

ARE YOU CONFIDENT©?

SATURDAY, JULY 14, 2007

EMPLOYEE RESEARCH

There is unease out there. Can you feel it?

Earlier this week, the Dow soared to a new record, gaining more in one day than in any other day in the last four years. The NASDAQ Composite Index also hit a six-year high. According to the U.S. Department of Labor, unemployment has held steady since September 2006 at between 4.4 and 4.6 percent, (a comparatively low figure), and in June, jobs (excluding farming) increased by 132,000. So why do I say that there is unease?

Sometimes, I sit here wondering if I am the only one worrying, and the rest of humankind thinks things are going along just swimmingly. Or do I represent the silent majority? I think I know the answer.

People are worried. What are the indicators? Approval ratings of congress are in the low-to-mid-teens. Approval ratings of the president are in the mid-twenties to low thirties. *The Wall Street Journal* reflects this unease about the recent stock market performance in its headline, "Dow Again Soars to Record High Despite Unease."

There are housing bubble and mortgage meltdown worries, energy cost worries, Iraq war worries and Iran building nuclear weapons and becoming increasingly unstable worries. There are concerns over a continuing erratic North Korea that at any moment might decide to lob a missile over Japan, sell nuclear material to others or simply collapse. There are defective and downright dangerous products and chemicals coming out of China (whose immediate solution was to execute the head of the country's version of the FDA). In one article, I am not sure if the author was trying to be humorous as he described how brushing your teeth should not be a death-defying act. (I was never religious about getting the last dab of toothpaste out of the tube, but now I find myself squeezing out every last bit, knowing that this tube did not kill me, but when I buy the next one, the result may be different).

People are worried about their jobs with continual outsourcing, offshoring, mergers and downsizing. Government reports indicate that Al Qaeda is increasingly trying to get back to pre-9/11 strength. Meanwhile, talking heads and spin-doctors try to persuade us that we are either better or worse depending on their political persuasion, and the public feels that they can't get a straight answer. We bravely wait for the inevitable terrorist attack to occur, and we just want to grab one of those terrorists by the scruff of the neck and scream at him or her to get a life as he or she schemes on how to take ours away.

Global warming is increasingly impacting us. Let's forget the debate about what is causing climate change and let's just deal with it—doing what we need to do to reduce its impact, help humanity survive it and leave our children a world in which they can live. I remember a speech given by John Browne, the former head of BP. I hope I don't butcher it, but I recall his position on global warming as being, "we can debate forever the impact of the chemicals we are putting into the air, but our activities are putting things into the air beyond what is naturally there, so lets do what we can to minimize it." Common sense environmentalism.

Blackstone's billionaires have found a way to beat the tax system. *The New York Times* quoted one regulator as saying, "they have found out how to make paying taxes an annuity." Once again, the little guy feels like he is left holding the bag. Business activities like this make you feel that business ethics are once again suspect and that everyone is out only for himself or herself. What is happening to our society? Oil is now trading at more than $70 per barrel and gas pump prices are in the mid-three dollar range, leaving consumers wondering how much higher they can go. The extra cost of the gallon, while painful, is livable for many. Yet the underlying worry is about the fragility of our oil supply, with every storm or maintenance issue causing imminent peril to our well-being and further price increases. What will happen next? Ahhhh, breathe…

In order to measure (somewhat scientifically) how the general population feels we are doing, a number of organizations conduct random polling, asking questions about current attitudes and events. One such index is the Consumer Confidence Index, which is tracked religiously, and significantly impacts the stock market and business decisions if its results take an unexpected turn. The various versions of consumer confidence indices try to predict future behavior of consumers and hence, potential outcomes for businesses. *The Wall Street Journal* and other media report on these indices regularly and even make announcements that "investors are anticipating the results of the latest poll due out next week."

It would seem that beyond insight into future consumer behavior, a good deal of useful information could be gained by asking employees their thoughts regarding the performance of their organizations (who better to ask than the people who work within them?) and their own personal future. I suggest that there is an additional measure that plugs a measurement hole that currently exists. It would provide additional insight and shed light on how we are doing and feeling as a country at the employee and organizational level. I suggest that in aggregate, if employees feel good about their respective organizations, then we as a nation will prosper. If they feel poorly, then we are headed in a direction that we would prefer not to be headed.

If we approach this correctly, it would be possible to create a worldwide standard that will become widely accepted and tracked by the media, and create a pull from organizations who would want to employ it. I propose that we begin to utilize a measure called Employee Confidence©.

The exact methodology employed in measuring Employee Confidence will be discussed elsewhere, but I believe we would find that engagement is a necessary, but not sufficient condition for Employee Confidence, which is strongly linked to certain business outcomes.

Employee Confidence has two main sub-components:
1. Organizational Confidence©
2. Personal Confidence©

Each of these components has an internal and external component.
- Organizational Confidence deals with ratings of the future of the organization in which the employee is a member (internal), and secondly, the future of the industry in which that organization operates (external).

- Personal Confidence deals with the employees' perception of their future at their current employer (internal), and (external) confidence in their skill set allowing them to find another job if they left the organization, regardless of the reason.

I believe this last component, Personal Confidence, has a large impact on how the future of employee loyalty will be defined and created.

Employee Confidence is something that I have been thinking about for some time, and I believe the time is ripe for further investigation and work in this area. Here is a sample of how it could be measured.

Employee Confidence Items[©]
Organizational Confidence

Internal

- My company is managed well and has effective business processes.
- My company produces high quality products or services.
- My company will likely be very successful financially over the next year.

External

- My company offers products or services that are attractive to our customers.
- My company has positioned itself well compared to competitors in our markets.
- The marketplace for my company's products or services is robust and healthy.

Personal Confidence

Internal

- I currently feel secure in my job.
- I feel that I have a bright long-term future with my company.
- My company is helping me develop the skills that I will need in the future.

External

- Should I leave my job, I feel well qualified and up-to-date in my skills to find another.
- Should I leave my job, I feel that equivalent opportunities would be available to me at other organizations.

RED CLOUD AND RONNIE

SUNDAY, JULY 1, 2007

JUST FOR KICKS

On the last full day of our family vacation, my daughter was interested in going horseback riding. We got a recommendation from our hotel's concierge, and off we went. My wife had taken my daughter down the Alpine Slide the day before while I stayed with Grandma, so it was my turn to have an experience with my seven-year old.

I may have been on a horse once before in my life, but somehow it seems very vague and distant. My only conclusion is that it must have been a memory that I have suppressed. I wonder what happened on that ride that I have no memory of it. So, it was with a mixture of excitement and trepidation that we lined up on the porch of the horse ranch, and the wrangler of our expedition started asking each of us about our riding experience. When he asked my daughter, I jumped in and said that this was her first time on a horse, as I wanted to make sure she got a nice gentle steed. He asked her if she wanted to ride by herself or if she wanted to have someone lead her horse. She answered with no hesitation, "I wanted to ride by herself." The wrangler then turned to me and asked about my riding experience. I did not want to brag about my vast riding experience as I wanted a gentle horse as well, so I indicated to him that I had seen a horse once—in a picture—and if he would just tell me where to insert the ignition key, I would be just fine. The wrangler, with a grin on his face, looked at me as though he had something in mind. "Ronnie for the sweet youngster," he yelled into the barn, "and Red Cloud for her dad."

Ronnie was the first to emerge from the barn. He looked like a nice, gentle horse with a small saddle just the right size for a seven-year old. My daughter jumped onto a stump that was there to give a boost up, and then in a blink of an eye, she was sitting in the catbird's seat, a big grin mixed with a small look of concern on her face. Red Cloud came next. He was big, about the size of my Grand Cherokee, and about the same color, too. I am sure I also had a look of concern on my face as I thought about how I was going to get on this animal. I wondered if I could just lead him on our walk. I am pretty sure I saw cowboys doing that in the movies, where in a tender moment of bonding, they walked by their horses heads, having conversations about where the next watering hole might be. But no, I was expected to perch on top. Without any shame, I decided to use the stump to help me get on the horse, as I wanted to make sure to avoid a groin injury in case the Yankees called on me to pitch in the next home game.

I swung my leg over and was surprised to find myself in the saddle rather than on the ground on the other side. Well, that wasn't too bad. How hard could the rest be? Red Cloud turned his head to look and see who was sitting on his back. He gave me a look that indicated he would appreciate it if I lost a few pounds. I scratched his neck in an effort to generate some good will. Red Cloud seemed to sense that I was a neophyte and decided immediately to take advantage. He took a few steps toward a mare that was standing by the fence. I thought this other horse must be a friend and he was just going over to say hello. Like a couple of old neighbors who hadn't seen each other in a few weeks, he was going over to chat about how their various rides had progressed. "Hey, how's it going?" Red Cloud would whinny. "I've got this chubby New Yorker on my back; you have any interesting riders lately?" And, she would whinny back, "No, not really." One of the wranglers, jerked me back to reality, "Keep Red Cloud away from that other horse," she shouted. "He is just trying to get *close* to her and is annoying her. See how her ears are pinned back? She is about to throw him a kick."

"Just great," I thought. I am going to be sitting on Red Cloud as he tries to mate with another horse. I had to ask what I should do to get Red Cloud to move away from his potential bride, and she yelled over, "Pull on the reins!" After a few futile attempts, a wrangler came over and led my horse away. So far so good. We were still in the yard not having begun our ride yet.

They lined us up. I was immediately behind my daughter who was beginning to look more and more comfortable in the saddle. We were second and third in line immediately after our guide, and off we went. We took what looked to be a narrow dirt path up the side of the hill and began climbing toward the ridgeline of the mountain range. I was expecting a nice tour for about an hour, but we began to climb through thickets and some wooden terrain. My daughter was now getting very comfortable, bouncing around in her saddle, yelling back to me to watch out for this obstacle or that one.

Red Cloud meanwhile had some other things on his mind—like eating grass at every opportunity. He knew who was boss and he knew that it wasn't me. I did, however, begin to get the hang of rein management—how to hold the reins in order to get the horse to do what I wanted. Sometimes it worked.

I noticed something. The path we were on was significantly worn; in fact, it was more like a rut. In some places, the rut was four inches or so below the rest of the ground, while at other points the rut was a good 12 inches below ground level. I thought to myself, "How many times have horses traveled this same path with tourists on their back?" I asked the guide at the head of the line if the horses could do the tour without any guide, given how many times they must have made the same trek. He answered affirmatively; he thought that most of the horses, if turned loose, would follow the script. Hmmm...I've got a horse so used to routine that it does not need a guide. What would happen if something out-of-the-ordinary happened? How would the horse respond? Should I put it to the test?

Just then, we broke out of the brush and found ourselves on the top of the ridgeline. We were treated to expansive views of spectacular wide-open plains with a stream meandering through about 1,000 feet below us. The guide yelled back that we were looking at the National Elk Refuge, winter home to approximately 5,000 or so elk. The view was out of this world, with abundant wild flowers around us, but the path was very narrow and should the horse fall, or just decide to brush me off, it was going to be a long way down. I decided it was time to come to some kind of understanding with Red Cloud. I indicated to him that if he kept me on his back and did not stumble on any of the rocks or tree roots in our path that I would not pull up on the reins the next time he wanted to stop for some grass. I thought that it was the least I could do for a horse that now had my life in his hands—or at least on his hoofs. Red Cloud turned his neck to look at me as I talked to him, and I am pretty sure that I saw him wink in the affirmative. A Faustian bargain had been reached.

We continued on our spectacular tour and I began to think about how organizations can get into ruts, running on autopilot in an extremely routine fashion. Along the way, companies might try to mate or merge with other organizations; they need sustenance in the form of products or services—both delivered to customers and received from suppliers. But even when operating in this fashion, they have the potential of delivering some spectacular results. But what happens when the non-routine occurs? I had to test that out still. The wrangler at the end of our column broke me out of my thoughts, when he yelled, "Pull up on Red Cloud's reins! Don't let him eat grass! He is slowing down the whole group." I apologized to Red Cloud and pulled him away from the grass he was munching on. Meanwhile, my daughter was having the time of her life, conducting a non-stop conversation with the guide regarding a host of nature related questions, including what animals he had seen on this trail. He indicated to her that in addition to sage grouse, elk and antelope, he had recently seen a moose. A moose! He, he now had my full attention.

We eventually ended up back at the ranch and as we entered the yard. The horses that we thought we were confidently in control of decided that they would wander to whatever point of interest they desired. Once they got out of their rut, they exhibited a good deal of free expression. Luckily for me, the mare was nowhere in sight. We got back into our car, after purchasing the obligatory horse riding photos, and my daughter stated very firmly that she could live here.

A Moose In The Distance

Friday, June 29, 2007

ORGANIZATIONS

What do organizations want? The answer is nothing. Organizations are nothing more than an abstraction. Organizations are virtual; they do not exist. You can't talk to an organization. You can't touch an organization. You can't expect an organization to operate in one fashion or another.

An organization is an amalgamation, a sum of its people. You can talk to an organization's people. You can shake hands with its people and you can expect its people to behave in a certain fashion.

So what do organizations want? They want whatever it is the people within the organization want. If the people in the organization desire to behave in a respectful way toward others, then the organization is known for respectful treatment. If the organization is one in which quality is paramount for each individual, then the organization becomes known for delivering quality products and services. The organization takes on the characteristics by which the majority of its people operate. (It is of course incumbent to the organization to provide the resources that people need in order to operate in the desired fashion).

What is the tipping point? Is it the point at which an organization's reputation is driven by those characteristics? Is it when a third of the people operate according to a certain shared vision? One-half? Two-thirds? I don't know an exact number, but I suspect that this number will vary somewhat depending on the characteristic that is being adopted. Unfortunately, what is very clear is that a negative characteristic is associated more easily with an organization's reputation than a positive one. It only takes a single breech of ethics to taint a reputation. A single quality issue can require an organization to constantly re-prove itself with a customer. A relatively minor labeling issue on a report, for instance, can cast the veracity of the whole report into doubt—doubt that is much more easily purchased than is a reputation of quality.

The notion of how an organization will operate, its standards, must percolate throughout the entire organization. Critical operating standards need to be infused into every aspect of organizational functioning. They need to break through any barriers that might exist as they find their way into each and every pocket of the organization. For instance, safety cannot be the imperative of a manufacturing unit and then overlooked elsewhere. Safety, an example used in this case, must be infused everywhere in the organization if it is to stick long-term within the organization and become part of what the organization is and how it is defined. This notion applies to all organizational characteristics by which the organization desires to be known and to build a reputation upon (e.g. customer focus, innovation, quality, cost control).

I have had an interest that I've been pursuing for a number of years. I have been hoping to see a moose in its natural habitat, and trips I have taken to Alaska, Vermont, Maine and Wyoming have been partially driven by my desire to observe a wild moose. I have been successful twice in my pursuit of this elusive creature—once in Alaska and once in Wyoming. But each time there has been a slight snag. The moose has been so far away from me that it was no more than a small dot, only visible by binoculars. The notion of being close enough to observe its behavior, to really feel its presence, to get a sense of what the creature is really like, has been slightly beyond my grasp each time. Each sighting has left me feeling somewhat unfulfilled. Somehow, those partial successes have only driven me to plan my next foray into moose observation with a little more intensity.

Just as the pursuit of a desire will often fall short of the vision of perfection in your head, the pursuit of the perfect organizational environment is also an elusive goal as well. There is no such thing as a perfect organization. There's only a vision of perfection to strive for—only to find that this vision is constantly somewhat just out of reach. But that doesn't mean we give up on our vision, our desires; we simply need to plan with a little more intensity for our next foray. We set goals. We set goals not because they represent an end state, but because they represent brief stops along the way. In today's competitive ever-changing environment, the eventual end state—the culmination of the dream—does not exist. The end goal is a moving elusive target, but one, we, as members of the organization, must pursue.

Work/Life Balance

MONDAY, JUNE 25, 2007

HUMAN RESOURCES

"From June 23rd to June 30th, I have retreated to a corner of the Grand Teton mountain range for a period of quiet reflection, an examination of my life situation and a rejuvenation of my spirit. I am available by email and by cell phone if you need to reach me."

What has happened to work/life balance? Did we ever really have it? Almost every technological improvement that has recently come our way—the things that were supposed to improve our quality of life and make our workloads easier—have resulted in more connectivity and the feeling that you can never get away. I wonder if the best answer is that we should stop trying to have a work/life balance.

Work/life balance implies that there is work and then separately that there is life—as though work needs to be kept in a separate box and not impinge on what is really important, namely life. A second aspect also emerges—that life is good and work is bad, and that the good must be balanced with the bad. Of course, this is not accurate.

When I have been asked about my workload, I find it very difficult to answer. A long time ago, I came to the realization that what I do for a living is a large part of who I am. What I do for a living is not kept in a separate box, only to be brought out between 9 a.m. and 5 p.m.—or between 7 a.m. to 7 p.m., as the case may be. What I do for a living is integrated into my being. I can work early in the morning, late in the evenings or on weekends, and not feel like I am working. What I am doing is what I do. As the saying goes, it is not an occupation, it is a lifestyle.

A conversation I often have with CEOs revolves around work/life balance. It usually focuses on the unrelenting pace that their organizations face and what can do to help people cope with the pace of change and work/life balance. This conversation is almost always prefaced with a caveat: "the workload and pace of change are not going away, in fact they are likely to increase, so don't tell me to not drive the organization as hard as we do."

A common question on employee surveys is, "I am able to maintain a good balance between my work and my personal life," again the notion of separation. I wonder if the definition of normalcy around this topic has already changed, but we are still asking about it with the old mindset. What if the question was reworded to, "I am able to effectively integrate my work and personal life." This takes what was a negatively connotative item and puts it into a positive framework. The goal of the organization is not to help the employee balance (which most were not really doing or were doing very poorly anyway), but to provide them with the tools and environment where an effective integration of the two is possible—creating the notion that working there is not a job, it is a lifestyle and a pretty good one at that.

If we can create the notion that work and personal life can be effectively integrated, rather than separated, a number of interesting workplace and homeplace options arise, some of which are already being utilized by organizations. The homeplace is an extension of the workplace and the workplace is an extension of the homeplace. There are certain activities that are better suited to the workplace and there are certain activities that are better suited to the homeplace, but there is also overlap. Some occupations and jobs have more overlap, and some have less, but that overlap almost always exists in one fashion or another.

I will be doing some rafting and canoeing on this trip. I wonder if I'll be able to respond to emails from a canoe on the Snake River.

Somewhere Else On The Continuum

Thursday, June 21, 2007

Organizations

Normal. What is it? Webster defines normal as, "according with, constituting, or not deviating from a norm, rule or principle," or as, "conforming to a type, standard or regular pattern." Some make fun of others being "normal," others make fun of people for not being normal. Some work diligently to be different, praising their abnormality as a virtue. Yet being "normal"—however it's viewed by their peers and the acceptance that flows from it—is what every adolescent inwardly strives for even if they don't really know what it is.

Rod Serling's series, "The Twilight Zone" aired an episode on November 11, 1960, called "Eye of the Beholder." The short story depicts a horribly disfigured woman who has had operation after operation in a desperate attempt to make herself beautiful, or at least, less disfigured and misshapen. This episode features her last attempt at a successful operation and shows her waiting impatiently in the hospital room until it is time to take off the bandages. Finally, the appointed time arrives. As the bandages fall away, she gazes into a mirror to see a stunningly beautiful face. A moment later, she screams horribly and collapses into an inconsolable heap on the floor. The camera pans around the room to reveal that everyone else in this "Twilight Zone" is, according to our standards, horribly misshapen. Yet being misshapen there is "normal." However, being normal is not really that simple.

Most things in life are not binary. You are not simply rich or poor, tall or short, fat or thin, beautiful or misshapen, sane or insane. You typically fall somewhere on the middle of a continuum. Most of us typically fall in the "fat" part of the normal distribution curve and are hence dubbed, "normal." What is abnormal though? Is abnormal one standard deviation from the mean, two standard deviations, or three? And what we define as abnormal has broad implications for those dubbed so. *The New York Times* in a June 19, 2007 article titled "States Face Decisions On Who Is Mentally Fit To Vote," describes two inmates, who, by reason of insanity, were found innocent of murder, but have been allowed to vote in elections. They were far enough out on the distribution (classified as abnormal) not to be held account-able for their crimes, and yet are not far enough out on the distribu-tion (classified as normal) to be prevented from voting. I could make a joke here, but I will bite my tongue. There is an implication here that is worth mentioning. Namely, you can be considered normal (within a certain distance from the mean) on one aspect of who you are, while being considered abnormal in another. If we were all so-ciopathic killers, then being a sociopathic killer would be normal—as difficult as it is for us to think that way.

The continuum of normal runs in both directions from the mean. Think for instance of cleanliness. Most of us are just average when it come to our compulsiveness for cleanliness. However, some of us are exceedingly sloppy, at the lower end of the continuum, and others of us are exceedingly fastidious, at the upper end of the continuum. Abnormality comes in two flavors, too much or too little of a characteristic.

Being classified as normal or abnormal does not just pertain to the individual level, but also pertains to the various levels of organiza-tional units that we humans create. When one culture defines a specific degree or a certain aspect of its society (an organizational unit) as normal, and a different culture defines that same degree or aspect as abnormal, there exists the potential for an explosive mix. For instance, the circumcision of women is considered abnormal in western culture and is often described as mutilation. Yet in other cultures, it is considered normal. Many in western cultures feel so strongly about this practice and its damage to women that they attempt to promulgate their standards of normalcy onto other cultures. In the United States, we find it difficult to understand why there is resistance to the common sense notion that mutilating women is wrong. While this extreme example makes it easier for us to say what is right and what is wrong (according to our own perspective), sometimes the choices we have to make are not so clear. Getting tattoos was once considered abnormal—an event that happened only to sailors when they got drunk. Our society, however, has changed the definition of what is normal when it comes to self-mutilation, tattoos and other body piercings, all of which are now much more commonly accepted.

There is another aspect to "normal" that affects organizations and needs to be examined. Does normal infer mediocrity? If an organization is like every other organization, how does it stand out from the crowd? How do you differentiate your product or service? In the case of organizational performance, is it good to be abnormal, at the high end of the distribution? I would argue so, but I would also argue that no organization has the resources, the time, energy, people or money to be an abnormally high performer in all aspects of its performance. Furthermore, a strategic issue for organizations to deal with is to decide the aspects of their performance in which they need to be abnormal—or to be politically correct, aspects in which to be world-class performers. Additionally, being at the high end of the distribution on certain aspects of performance negates the ability to be high on other aspects of performance. For instance, if the organization is to be the most customer focused, highest in quality and most innovative, it is quite difficult to be the lowest cost provider. In essence, it is a contradiction. To be the lowest cost, the organization would need to sacrifice services in order to meet that goal—sacrifices that affect the ability to be the most customer focused, most innovative and highest in quality.

But there is a special case here—a situation that if the organization can create it, it will cause substantial rewards to accrue. That is, control of the definition of normalcy. What is defined as normal is a moving target. What was once abnormal can be shifted in perception and made part of the mainstream, part of normalcy. If an organization that is operating in a normal fashion can successfully implement a transformational change, redefining not only itself, but the definition of normal from a product or process perspective, the company can control the market for that service or product. FedEx redefined the speed at which a package can be delivered, and controlled the market. It created a new definition of normal, the standard by which everyone else is judged. I no longer had to wait two to three days for a package delivery; I could get it there overnight. Apple created a new definition of the normal way in which we bought and listened to music. Ford created a new definition of affordability for the automobile, creating a new normal for who could own a car. The Japanese car companies redefined what "normal" quality levels were. We are not simply talking about innovation here. We are talking about the kind of innovation that redefines a market and causes a shift in definition—the definition of what is normal. Unfortunately, many companies are not up to the challenge, but for those that can change that definition—establishing a new normal—the potential rewards are enormous.

Organizational Entropy

Tuesday, December 19, 2006

Organizations

Organized systems want to operate with the lowest level of energy expenditure possible; it seems to be the natural state not only of living organisms, but of our human organizational creations as well. Some animals, for instance, are nocturnal in order to conserve energy and not exhaust themselves during the hot part of the day. Other animals follow strategies that allow them to endure tough times by hibernating. The "procedures" these animals follow are strategies to help them cope with their environment.

Human organizations also put into place rules and procedures by which they will operate to help them cope with their environment. The purpose of these rules is to allow the organization to make decisions using "standard operating procedures" as a guideline and hence, remove from the organization the need to "think" about the decisions being made. For an organization to think, time and resources are required—an expenditure of energy.

Removing the need to "think" about some decisions carries an inherent risk—the risk of mediocrity or worse, the risk of extinction. In order to make decisions in a routine fashion, organizations try to come up with a solution that prevents the worse case scenario, that works in most situations and that fits the largest number of people in the largest number of circumstances. I think that organizations, however, often make up rules for the smallest part of the distribution—those at the bottom tail end.

It has been shown time and again that for a given behavior within an organization, a normal distribution of that behavior will occur. For instance, some people will never take sick days, others will take a few each year (when they are sick) and a small percentage will find any reason (a sniffle, a headache, the feeling of getting sick) to avoid coming into work.

Organizations have a tendency to count. It's easy. They may say, "Here is the number of sick days you are allowed," rather than creating a rule that says if you are sick, stay home. Or if you are well, come to work—and then manage the people who abuse the system. Are the rules that the organization puts into place for the average person? Or are they for those at the bottom tail of the distribution? Interestingly, organizations will espouse the one rule as policy—here is your number of sick days—then operate according to the other. It becomes a way of saying, "gotcha" for those that abuse the system, but it actually shows a lack of respect for the majority and a lack of desire to inject energy into organizational decision making—the kind of energy needed to deal with those outside of acceptable parameters.

For any circumstance that is outside of the range of responses the organization has based its procedures on, you run the risk of the decision not being optimal for that situation or the particular person. Yet many organizations slavishly apply these "solutions" to everyone. The outcome of this is to force standard or average solutions on potentially non-average circumstances. As organizations grow, they adopt more of these solutions to help handle the increased number of decisions that need to be made. Bureaucracy is a form of organizational entropy.

In organizations where management is not working harmoniously, these solutions can be a defense mechanism, allowing feuding managers to avoid interacting with each other. By having a standard set of rules, we don't have to talk, to engage. We can simply let the organization run itself—right into the ground.

For living organisms, when a non-average, out-of-range situation occurs, disrupting the routine, there is the potential for great risk, including potential extinction. Will the polar bear, now faced with global warming, be able to cope with the lack of ice floes at the North Pole? Ice floes that "procedure" says are used to hunt seals? Can the polar bear now adapt to a non-average environment—one that is out of its range of experience—or will it continue to try to apply standard operating procedure and face possible extinction?

Here is an assumption about people at work. I have yet to see any evidence that contradicts this assumption, and have seen significant evidence that supports it. In general, most employees want to do a good job at work. There is a small portion of employees who do not fit this description, and unfortunately, organizations generally create rules for this subset rather than the majority. Organizations manage for the exception. Isn't it ironic that the "average" person wants to do a good job, and yet our organizations create procedures not to deal with the average, but to deal with the outliers, the exceptions? These rules are then often indiscriminately applied to everyone. Does this mean that our organizations are less fit than their natural counterparts are? Are we less or more resilient when the normal situation shifts?

Humans of course are only doing what comes naturally. In order to make decision making easier, we have a tendency to categorize people into groups, to create stereotypes. These stereotypes are not only often wrong; they do a tremendous injustice to those who have been categorized. Categorization is a way for a person to use less energy, to avoid thinking about the decisions being made. This behavior, at the individual level, will at best lead to mediocrity, or bigotry, as well as missed opportunities to enjoy the rich diversity of the human state of being. Organizations, made up of human beings with frailties, make the same mistake; they paint with a broad brush.

A Rabbi that I greatly admire wrote in a recent editorial, "...generalizations are dehumanizing. The most amazing and indisputable characteristic about our humanness is that each of us is unique...Sameness is a delusion. Sameness is contrary to nature and destructive of the human spirit." He speaks of the same human spirit that organizations need to tap into to unlock their potential. What can be done in organizations to avoid this pitfall?

First, let's take a lesson from state-of-the-art manufacturing. Mass customization allows a consumer to tailor a product within a given set of parameters to fit his or her needs. Instead of sitting on the shelf, the products are manufactured as needed to fill the specific order and the specific need. The use of technology allows the orders to be completed in a fashion and at speed similar to traditionally mass produced items. The days of "you can have it in any color you want as long as that color is black" are rapidly disappearing. I believe this concept of mass customization can be successfully applied to our organizational policies and practices—not just to manufacturing.

Secondly, organizations need to examine what they actually reward. It is well known that organizations get the behavior they actually reward, not necessarily what they espouse. Supervisors are given recognition rewards to distribute to their employees, but these same supervisors are rewarded for coming in under budget. How do you come in under budget? One way is to not to give out the recognition rewards! It is often a very healthy exercise for an organization to review what they are actually rewarding.

Third, we have to be prepared to inject a bit of energy into our organizations to overcome the natural tendency toward organizational entropy. Sometimes it is simply a matter of willingness (and not killing the messenger) to run non-routine situations up the line. Even better, with the appropriate people in place, it's simply driving down the decision making process so the non-routine can be handled locally. I have been in many organizations where running something up the line, if it happens often, is not good for one's career—the classic case of organizational entropy.

Fourth, people learn lessons from having average solutions applied to them, and shift toward the center of the distribution in terms of the way they interact and deal with the organization. They, just like the polar bear, learn to deal with the average situation by behaving in a certain way. We need to encourage diversity of behavior and procedure so that when the situation is no longer average, we can adapt. I term this the "cautious embrace of variance."

What about all that hard work we do? It certainly feels like we spend a lot of energy here getting things done. Yes, that is true. People work very hard in organizations, but I want to draw a distinction between people in organizations working hard and organizations seeking to operate with low expenditures of energy. Living systems get an "energy" input that creates order only to begin a run down to lower energy states (disorder). This happens until more energy is put into the system from the outside. Food or fuel is taken in to re-energize the system. But some animals, to increase their odds of survival, fill a niche that is unoccupied by others, which may require greater expenditures of short-term energy.

That means that organizations to the extent possible like to run on autopilot, without thinking about the "routine" decisions being made. How much can one spend on a meal when you travel? Do you fly coach or business class? Who can pull the lever and stop the production line? Can a salesperson authorize a discount? Who can commit to a client deadline? How many sick days do you get? How many vacation days?

Can organizations learn from nature? Can they learn from those animals that occupy niches, which may require more energy use but lead to greater survival odds? I think so, but they will have to expend some energy to do so.

A study, reported on in July 2007, indicated that polar bear mothers, to a much greater extent, are now creating their winter birthing dens on land rather than on ice floes. This is in response to the lack of suitable ice floes for dens forming over the winter months in which they give birth and protect their cubs from the arctic winter. While this adaptation inspires some hope that polar bears are learning to cope with the changing situation, by necessity, they are not out of the woods and will likely be listed as endangered. The good news is that they are adapting just as we will be required to adapt to the Earth's changing climatic conditions. Let's hope that their adaptation enable polar bears to survive.

The above text was added in September 2007.

The Meaning Of Leadership - Part I

Thursday, May 24, 2007

Performance

It is unusual, but I can remember very clearly, my first act of meaningful leadership. I was working my way through college by doing three 24-hour shifts a week on the local ambulance. We were the only certified heart mobile in the county, and I was an emergency cardiac care technician with advanced trauma certification. I had a lot of practice taking care of people, doing 15 calls on a busy shift. I was often so tired the next day that after class, I fell asleep in the library while trying to study.

New Years Day, 1979. It was a bone chilling night, and we were returning to our bunkhouse (calling it a house is being generous as it was the back end of a run-down auto supply store) from a routine call where we had just dropped the patient off at Lourdes Hospital. It was about 2 a.m. We heard our radio go off and alert us that a car had just plunged off the Court Street Bridge into the Susquehanna River. That was less than a half mile in front of us. I was riding shotgun and my partner was driving. We turned on the lights and siren and he stepped on it. We were the first to arrive on the scene. The river was partly frozen as it had been a fairly cold winter so far. The car was near the bank and was only partly submerged where it had broken though the ice. I leapt out of the ambulance and grabbed my trauma kit through the side door. I was able to slide down the embankment next to the bridge to reach the car, which was about 30 or 40 feet below me.

When I got to the car, I opened the door where I found two women. Upon examination, I was sure they both had broken necks and were not breathing. In my trauma kit, I had one esophageal obterator airway, which worked well in situations like this. You pass a tube into the patient's esophagus and inflate a balloon at the end of the tube to prevent the contents of the stomach from coming up. This also creates a seal, allowing you to pass air into the lungs, through holes in the tube, at the level of the epiglottis, by way of the trachea. I began to work on one woman establishing an airway and pumping air into her lungs with an ambu bag. I checked for a pulse on both women. They were both alive and one was now "controlled" as I assisted her breathing.

My hands were full, and unfortunately, I had left my mobile radio in the ambulance in my hurry to get down the embankment. I still had one patient in the car who was not breathing and I did not have another obterator with me. Meanwhile, the fire department had arrived and they were standing around at the top of the bridge deciding on the best course of action. At the time, I was carrying a five-cell cast aluminum flash light that had quite a bit of heft to it and put out a very bright light (it came in handy ocassionaly on Saturday night ambulance runs). I considered myself then—and still do today—to be a fairly shy and introverted person. I never before had issued commands to someone much older than me, but I pulled out my flashlight and shined it into the eyes of the nearest firefighter who looked like he had some authority. Then I said in the most command-ing voice I could muster, "I have two women down here with broken necks, who are not breathing. I need some more supplies from my ambulance and I need it now or they are going to die." All of a sud-den, I had 20 people doing what I needed them to do. I was a college kid, and yet I was coordinating the activity of many older people. I was actually surprised that I was able to pull it off, getting all those firefighters to do as I said.

I got the rest of my equipment lowered down on a rope, and my partner was able to leave the ambulance and join me. I carefully inserted an obterator in the second woman; we then secured their necks, started IVs so we could pass meds if necessary and eventually were successful in assisting their breathing. Starting IVs for two women with broken necks in a partially submerged car was no small trick. With the help of the fire department, we placed them on backboards and into wire baskets so they could be raised out of the river. They were placed in the back of my ambulance. The fire department had lowered an aluminum ladder into the river for my partner and me to use. Given the work I was doing, I had taken off my gloves earlier, so I climbed out on the ladder bare handed. I hurried to the ambulance where we continued to care for the two women.

We took the women to Binghamton General Hospital, which was the nearest hospital to where we were. It was only after we had successfully delivered them to the emergency room that we took stock of ourselves. I was soaking wet up to my knees and my hands began hurting incredibly. I had frost bite on my hands from climbing out on a metal ladder that was immersed in the river water, and was now feeling the effects as my hands warmed up. We were both tended to by the ER staff.

For me, this instant crystallized one important aspect of what being a leader means. When you know you are right, act on it. When you can get others to see things from your point of view and they can assist you, you greatly magnify your leverage. This moment also put many other things into perspective for me. As I began my consulting career, my peers would wonder why I was not nervous speaking in front of important CEOs or large groups of people. I would look at them and I would remember the two women in the river and think about what was really important in life. We are all accumulations of our experiences. Because of this, I have a tendency to speak my mind now, to get tired easily with minutia and have trouble putting any kind of veneer on situations.

A few days later, I went to visit the women in the hospital and that is when my youthful bubble of exuberance was really burst. Both women were still alive and both would recover. They had screws placed into their skulls that were fastened to braces to prevent any head movement. The one woman, who was the driver, started screaming at me, as best she could with her head pinned, "What right did you have to save my life! Why didn't you just let me die?" Apparently, the driver had decided to commit suicide and had decided to take her friend with her. I could not bring myself to go back to see her again. I only hoped that later on she would have a change of heart.

THE MEANING OF LEADERSHIP – PART II
& THE ORGANIZATIONAL MIDDLE CLASS

FRIDAY, JUNE 1, 2007

PERFORMANCE

"…We cannot dedicate, we cannot consecrate, we cannot hallow this ground.
The brave men, living and dead, who struggled here, have consecrated it,
far above our poor power to add or detract. The world will little note, nor long
remember what we say here, but it can never forget what they did here."
–Abraham Lincoln, 1863, The Gettysburg Address

Organizations need to foster the development of a strong, vibrant middle class of employees as a mechanism to help them successfully compete in today's turbulent marketplace. The workers that make up this organizational middle class are the warriors by which the organization will either flourish or flounder. These workers will determine if the organization can endure. It is incumbent upon the organization to prepare employees and equip them properly for battle. What does this mean and how can this be done? There are some lessons to be learned by an examination of the behaviors of America's founding fathers.

The Value of Education

One of the essential elements for a strong, vibrant, lasting democracy to exist is the establishment of a sizeable middle class—a middle class, by definition, that is not struggling day-to-day to meet its essential needs of food, housing and healthcare. One major way of helping to create a strong middle class is through education. The U.S. has been the benefactor of a relatively strong educational system since almost the start of the union, and even today, it has an advanced educational system that is the envy of the world. There are, however, many different models of educational systems. For organizations, a primary challenge is to determine the educational model that is best for their circumstances.

Thomas Jefferson, a founding father of the United States, was also the founding father of the University of Virginia. He began the institution with the notion that the university should train a new leadership-elite based on selecting individuals by their virtues and talent. While he clearly did not believe in inherited opportunities, he did seem to feel that people should be selected based on their talents and skills and then should be provided an opportunity for a fine education. This, in essence, created a new intellectual class of ruling elites, albeit a class distinction that was not assured to pass through to future generations in the lineage, but one that was based on merit. To help assure that this education was not based on class, the university education was proposed to be provided to those who qualified for free.

Benjamin Franklin took a different approach. He also was a founding father of a university, the University of Pennsylvania. His goal was not to select promising young men for leadership based on merit, but to provide an education for all who wanted one. Viewing a broadly educated population as critical to the future success of the nation, he felt that if individuals wanted to learn, they should be welcomed there. Each individual, through his or her hard work and efforts, had a chance for an education. Franklin's idea was not one of creating a new meritocracy, but of providing an education for a broad array of individuals from all occupations and all walks of life. Today the reputation of the University of Pennsylvania is unsurpassed for providing an excellent education, and it also turns out many fine leaders.

In 1749, Benjamin Franklin penned the *Proposals Relating to the Education of Youth in Pennsilvania-Philadelphia,* which provided insight into his thinking about education when he stated, "That we may obtain the Advantages arising from an Increase of Knowledge, and prevent as much as may be the mischievous Consequences that would attend a general Ignorance among us, the following Hints are offered towards forming a Plan for the Education of the Youth of Pennsilvania." Franklin goes on to describe how schools should operate, how students should eat frugally and exercise frequently and what subjects should be specifically taught.

Benjamin Franklin was of the mind that leadership within the new nation could come from anywhere, that all people are created equal and should have an equal opportunity to make what they desire with their lives. He saw the benefit in having a highly educated population by implementing an educational system that provided wide access to all. Leaders, in his thinking, came from highly educated, motivated and intelligent common people. The same kind of people that Abraham Lincoln in the Gettysburg address would later say created our "government of the people, by the people, for the people..."

The contrast between creating a workforce that consists of a highly trained, small cadre of a select few versus a broadly educated workforce where everyone has a chance to achieve is a choice that must be made. Inherently, a broadly educated workforce is more flexible to changing environmental conditions, which makes the organization more resilient to external factors—a payback well worth the investment. A broadly educated workforce that has a strong emphasis on diversity also allows individuals with different backgrounds to propose new ideas or see unique solutions to the same problem, allowing the organization to examine alternatives in a rigorous fashion. And as

The spelling of Pennsilvania with an "i" is based on Benjamin Franklin's writings in 1749.
Because it is quoted material, this document has preserved the original text.

Benjamin Franklin points out, ignorance usually leads to unfortunate consequences and behaviors.

The Engaged Voter/Worker

There were a number of times in the mid-to-late-1800s that turnout for the U.S. presidential elections exceeded 80 percent of eligible voters. In 2000, the U.S. voter turnout for the presidential election was just over 50 percent, and was just below 60 percent in 2004. The U.S. population of the mid-19th century was highly engaged in political discussions and widely debated public issues. The issues of the day facing the country were of great importance, and each American knew that the way issues were decided could dramatically impact their day-to-day lives.

A major disconnect today is how little we perceive that the decisions in Washington affect our day-to-day lives. For instance, how many of us can say that we have been directly touched by the Iraq war? Where are the war bonds that were used to finance the war effort, as was done in WWII? Where is the draft that reached (theoretically) into potentially each and every household? It is no longer the majority of the population, but only a small segment that is affected by war, making the decisions from Washington seem less relevant to each of us. When Representative Charles Rangel talks about reinstituting the draft, he does so not only because the current system creates a disproportionate number of minorities in the military, but also because it restores the sense that if we are at War (with a capital W), it should be felt by the entire nation. He does so because as decisions are made about a war, they are made with the notion that they will be felt by the nation as a whole. War is thought about a little harder when it may be your children asked to fight.

In the 1800s, the speech was the major method of political communication from candidates or office holders. The great majority of newspapers—upon reporting on the speeches and issues—were described as highly partisan in their respective publications. Publishers, too, often had political ambitions. The news as unbiased reporting, in the spirit of Cronkite and Murrow, may have been an anomaly, and my perception of today's partisan reporting (and I have to add mostly trivial) may be more the historical norm.

If we were to look at the employee population of an organization, and they scored over 80 percent favorable on outcome items commonly used to measure employee engagement, we would say that the organization is doing quite well. And while not at the absolute highest possible levels of engagement, the company would be very, very solid. Organizations scoring just over 50 percent or just below 60 percent are in trouble. They have workforces that have lost or are losing enthusiasm, and clearly, for whatever the reason, maybe the workforce is not doing everything it can to help the organization succeed. If we look at voter turnout as a surrogate for voter engagement, we would say that the country was politically and organizationally healthier in the 1800s than it is today. Voter apathy, which is more prevalent today, is a potential sign of a disengaged or disengaging population—not a good state of affairs.

A vibrant middle-class workforce in organizations must be engaged and feel that it has a vital role in contributing to the decisions being made by the organization. The workforce must also feel that those decisions have the potential of affecting individuals on a day-to-day basis. It is difficult to engage a workforce if what is happening around it is viewed as having little to no importance to each member personally. The decisions of the organization should not affect only a small cadre of elites or small pockets scattered through the organization. If the organization is feeling pain, it should be generally felt throughout the organization, and if the organization is feeling success, likewise.

The King

George Washington could have been anointed king of the new nation—this new organization, had he so chosen—but he saw the benefits of another path. He did not see himself as a king, but as one of the common people in the newly emerging democracy. In relative humility, he chose to limit himself to two terms as president. He also chose, in his wisdom, to implement the parts of the constitution that called for the separation and relative equalization of power between the three branches of government. His choices enshrined him as one of the greatest presidents this nation has ever had.

The CEO can be thought of as the king of the organization. *The New York Times* (May 25, 2007) described the widening gulf between CEO pay and the pay levels of the organizational middle class and other elites in the organization only one or two levels below the CEO. This article titled, "More Than Ever, It Pays To Be The Top Executive," seems to describe a characteristic that some CEOs have developed or have fallen victim to. This notion, which George Washington was able to avoid, is that it is "good to be king." Moreover, some CEOs perceive themselves not of the common people, but rather that they should grab as much reward for themselves as possible.

CEOs today, often with the assistance of the Board of Directors, are creating a new isolated category based on the assumption that CEOs have some kind of special quality not commonly found. The article describes in some detail the establishment of a new small elite of very wealthy individuals, including sports figures, movies stars and CEOs. Will the choices of many CEOs today enshrine them as great leaders of their respective organizations? Or will history view them as the modern version of newspaper publishers from the 1800s, trying to fulfill personal ambition and greed?

A vibrant organizational middle class must be equitably compensated for their contributions. People who are worried about putting food on the table, making a mortgage payment or worrying about their car breaking down are not concentrating on the things that are important to the organization. There is a Russian saying, "I pretend to work, you pretend to pay me." This represents the bottom of a downward, deleterious cycle that needs to be reversed in creating a vibrant organizational middle class. Interestingly, pay is often a driver of engagement only when pay is low. As soon as pay hits an adequate level, creating an organizational middle class, it is no longer important and drops out as a driver. People who are poorly paid or view themselves as not equitably treated tend to be unengaged.

Organizational Democracy

If we review some of the most successful, widely admired organizations today, we begin to notice a common characteristic: they tend to have a vibrant organizational middle class. They are organizations that make the most out of their intellectual capital—intellectual capital gathered from their highly engaged workers.

Clearly, organizations are not democracies, but I think both can each learn a bit from the other. Democracies have been described as messy and difficult at getting anything done. But they have overwhelming positive characteristics and benefits for those societies willing to put in the hard work of creating and sustaining them. Creating a collaborative environment where people are highly engaged is not an easy thing. Organizations have a lot of moving parts, and maximizing the effectiveness of those parts is not easy. Accomplishing things that are not easy is part of what leadership is about. True leaders have the ability to bring the organization along with them as the entire organization accomplishes jointly held, aspirational goals.

> *"We choose to go to the moon. We choose to go to the moon in this decade and do the other things, not because they are easy, but because they are hard, because that goal will serve to organize and measure the best of our energies and skills, because that challenge is one that we are willing to accept, one we are unwilling to postpone, and one which we intend to win…"*
> *– JFK, September 12, 1962, Rice University*

Senator Charles Sumner, while speaking at Abraham Lincoln's funeral, stated that Lincoln was mistaken when he said "the world will little note, nor long remember what we say here." He stated, "The world noted at once what he said, and will never cease to remember it. The battle itself was less important than the speech."

THE MEANING OF LEADERSHIP - PART III: LEADERSHIP AND MANAGEMENT

WEDNESDAY, JUNE 6, 2007

PERFORMANCE

"We must make use of books on the subject of administration, especially the management studies and theories which have been recently published, since they are consonant with the nature of modern societies. There is more than one site on the Internet in which one can obtain management books."
- Abu Bakr Naji, The Management of Savagery (Al Qaeda leadership guide)

Mr. Abu Bakr Naji has written an extensive publication on leadership from the perspective of Al Qaeda. In a section on page 25 of his manuscript titled, "Who Leads, Who Manages and Who Authorizes the Fundamental Administrative Decisions?" he states:

'Not every leader is a manager and not every manager is a leader.' If we were to abide by what we mentioned in the previous point, we should change (this phrase) into, 'Every leader is a manager but not every manager is a leader.' The manager or executive is any individual within the movement or the group—who has mastered the art of administration—who can be appointed to manage a financial or nutritional sector or the like without him knowing, to the extent possible, the secrets which would harm the work. And as for the leader, he must be the object of complete reliance within the movement, and entrusted with its actions and its secrets... Therefore, in our plan we open the door of management wide to those who have mastered its art. As for the door of leadership, it is only open to those who are reliable, even though there is a security apparatus which keeps watch over the two doors, monitoring

the professionalism of the actions of the leaders and the managers in order to prevent infiltration. (Translated by William McCants. Funding for this translation provided by the John M. Olin Institute for Strategic Studies at Harvard University).

The definition of leadership and its relationship to management has been extensively studied and debated for a very long time. It is a question that each organization has to grapple with, including those we might not think of as dealing with these issues, such as Al Qaeda. That they have risen to this level of sophistication makes them all that much more dangerous.

In "Leading From Below" (*The Wall Street Journal,* March 3-4, 2007), James Kelly and Scott Nadler describe the necessity for companies to create environments that allow for and encourage leadership from below—the notion is that change needs to come from those managers below the "C" suite. They indicate that while the image survives of the all-powerful CEO, who is able to change the organization in a heartbeat, the reality is that due to investor and analyst demands, the ability of individuals at the senior most levels to introduce change is becoming more limited. They describe how managers below the "C" level can develop themselves—take risks—to influence the course of the organization and to implement change.

Larry Moses, president of the Wexner Foundation, an organization that studies and helps to foster leadership, in prepared remarks, goes further. He indicates that the goal of the organization should be to encourage each member to see his or her potential and to become a leader. He distinguishes very clearly between management (people who are in positions of authority with the mandate to get things executed) and leadership. He defines a leader as one who can mobilize others to adapt to change. In his words, "leadership is about changing immutable practices that have become obsolete." He believes that organizations need to foster environments where every member feels that he or she can and should lead. Managers can be leaders, but not every leader need be a manager.

What do we know about management and leadership from an employee survey perspective? In my view of organizational cultural assessment, management is about enabling people, providing them with what they need to get their jobs done. It is not about control; it is about creating and sustaining the conditions that allow people to excel. The commonly used survey item "XYZ is an effectively managed well-run organization," is most closely linked to people's frustration or lack thereof in their ability to get their jobs done. When people are frustrated in this area, invariably the organization scores poorly on being effectively managed. When people feel efficacious, the management of the organization is viewed positively. Leadership is discussed when speaking of vision. For instance, the item "Senior management of the organization has communicated a vision of the future that is motivational and creates passion in me" is about leadership. It's also about where the organization is headed and where the individual fits into that vision. It is not specifically about, "Do you have what you need to get your job done," which is about management.

Clear distinctions between leadership and management are drawn, but clearly, a senior manager has the potential for being a very effective leader. Where we sometimes lose our way is when we automatically equate management and positions of execution with leadership. Leadership is different from management. But what about the characteristics of leaders and managers? Is it the same or are there different skill sets? Warren Bennis, an industrial/organizational psychologist and one of the most quoted experts on leadership, states that, "Leadership is about doing the right things; management is about doing things right." One website devoted to this topic lists out the following characteristics of managers and leaders:

MANAGERS	LEADERS
restricting	enabling
controlling	freeing
playing safe	risking
molding	releasing
forcing	enhancing
regimenting	challenging
stifling	participating
rigid	flexible
autocratic	democratic
consistent	predictable

To me, the list is interesting, but more than a little simplistic and perhaps misleading. Not all managers are restricting or controlling, and if they are not, this doesn't necessarily make them a leader. If we took this list at face value, it would mean that leaders and managers are in essence opposites, which we know is not true. Many managers are great leaders and many leaders are also great managers. Dr. Bennis, in his book called "Leaders – Strategies for Taking Charge," criticizes much of the earlier work done on leadership because it simply places leadership as one of the tasks of being a manager. He argues that leaders serve a different purpose in the organization and are in need of a differing set of skills from a manager.

Perhaps what is not on the above list of leadership characteristics is most interesting to me. Yet in my work, these characteristics have proven to be the essence of leadership. Critical components of leadership are trustworthiness, ethics, intelligence and vision, as well as the ability to communicate that vision, the desire to create something lasting and focusing on what needs to be done to help others in the organization succeed over oneself. There are, of course, other critical elements. Leaders need not be perfect in all areas, as they, like the rest of us, are human. Yet some elements are zero tolerance issues— when a leader violates trust or breaches ethical practice he or she forsaken his or her leadership position and it cannot be regained.

Leadership and management positions are challenging occupations and tasks. We need to understand them to create conditions that allow our managers and leaders to succeed. There is always a feeling that we need to run faster, to do more in this area, and I think that is true as our enemies are right behind us studying and learning just as hard.

GARDEN PATHS AND
ORGANIZATIONAL MEMORY

MONDAY, MAY 21, 2007

ORGANIZATIONS

> *"How fair is a garden amid the toils and passions of existence."*
> *- Benjamin Disraeli*

Dick Cavett, the 1970s TV talk show host, has been writing a column for *The New York Times*, recently. In one of his columns, Dick described an incident where a guest died during the taping of one of his shows. The guest, a health food expert, died in front of the cameras, but because the show was taped, the episode never aired. Yet in his article, Mr. Cavett indicates that about 20 times per year, he has a conversation that goes something like this:

> "'Hey, Dick, I'll never forget the look on your face when that guy died on your show.'"
> I'm never sure exactly how to answer. Let's call the speaker "Don." Usually it goes on:
> Don: 'I'll never forget that.'
> D.C.: 'Ah, you were in the audience?'
> Don: 'No, I saw it.'
> D.C. (Uneasy): 'Well, you see that show never aired.'
> Don: 'C'mon, you're kiddin' me.'
> D.C.: 'It's true. And you're just one of a lot of people who are so sure that they saw it that they could pass a polygraph test.'
> Don: 'How did I see it then?'

D.C.: 'I hate to spoil your fun, but the only way you might have seen it is if you knew a couple of ABC engineers who ran off a copy that night to take home to spook their wives and girlfriends.'

Don: (With an expression that says, "Why are you pretending I didn't see it?") 'But I just know I saw it.'

D.C.: (Now trying to comfort poor Don who has had a cherished memory threatened): 'Maybe I described it so vividly the next night that you thought you actually saw it … and it was in all the papers and on the late news shows.'"

What do we remember and why? How accurate are our recollections? Saying that human memory is a very complicated thing makes me guilty of gross understatement. One aspect of the ability to recall a memory is thought to be related to the number of cross-references to a specific memory that exists within the brain. If you think of the brain as a vast filing system with hyperlinks, the more locations that you can come across with a hyperlink directing you to more information about a memory, the easier it is to recall that memory in detail. If a memory is isolated with little or no cross-references, it is more difficult to recall. Other senses can help evoke memory recall as well, as part of that cross-reference system. A certain smell, taste or a touch of a familiar object for instance can trigger vivid recall of an incident from long ago. (If only organizations could get you to smell their freshness and touch their innovativeness, it would be easier and more likely that you would recall those characteristics when thinking of them). If you think of the brain as a muscle, regular mental exercise, it has been shown, can help it work better.

How do organizations remember things? Is there such a thing as organizational memory stored in the organizational brain? What mental exercises can an organization do to keep its brain and its memories sharp, preventing them from fading into oblivion? If we think of the individual people within the organization as neurons, then the collective group of individuals within the organization is the brain. The sum total of knowledge, skills and abilities that these individuals possess represent the organization's knowledge and its memory. The organization, stripped of its neurons, has no innate ability; it only has a frame in which its component parts can exist. The employees of an organization, who breathe life into the organization also represent the logic, feelings and emotions of the organization; organizational surveys can be thought of as a tool or a sensory organ allowing us to see inside—just as an MRI does for human brains—the intricate organizational brain. Surveys give us only one view, however, just as our eyes can see visible light, but are blind to other wavelengths in the electromagnetic spectrum. Unfortunately, some of the things that our eyes can't see, such as radiation or an untrustworthy executive out for only personal gain, can kill you.

Some areas of our brain and our organizations have specialized functions that if damaged, can be taken over by other areas of the brain over time, and some areas, if damaged beyond repair, represent lost functionality.

Organizations work very hard at helping customers remember them; branding is very important for an organization that is trying to be easily remembered. What about things the organization itself needs to remember? Things like who it is, what it stands for, what principles will guide it, how it will operate and how it will treat employees. Internal branding can go a long way toward helping the organizational members remember what the organization is about and how it should operate. Can organizations have faulty memories, like the people who are so sure they saw that person die on Dick Cavett? Or are these just faulty perceptional organs?

One way to help the organizational members more easily remember is to cross-reference, the same process that our brain uses. In this case, what we are cross-referencing is all of the policies and practices that the organization has stated it will operate under, making sure that these all match up with the stated internal brand. The more that polices and practices—each one of them—are congruent with stated objectives, the more cross-references exist. For example, if the company stands for safety or quality or customer service, to help the organization remember it, all of the policies and practices need to be aligned to allow the employees to perform in a quality fashion, or safely, or in a customer focused fashion congruent to those objectives. Many organizations will state one thing and then by practice, send a different message to employees, destroying the ability to have an organizational memory.

One finding that I find somewhat remarkable in survey research is how consistent some organizational cultures can be—even organizations that are experiencing more than 100 percent turnover per year. How can it be in organizations where essentially every year there is 100 percent turnover that the culture remains consistent?

First, there is the error in how the turnover is measured. In these organizations, there is not 100 percent turnover, representing a change in all staff, but rather there may be 200 percent or more turnover among certain job categories (maybe an entry level position), and other categories such as management may have much lower turnover, providing a source of cultural consistency for the organization. Second, there is the organizational framework—the strategies, polices and practices that the organization adopts. For instance, an organization that is a low-wage paying organization, paying well below market, does not suddenly change its pay strategy because of turnover (although if the pain of losing good people, defined as the opportunity cost of turnover, is becoming greater than the perceived benefit of low wages, it may reconsider its strategy). Because the framework is consistent and in place for a low-wage environment, the next set of employees entering the organization experience the same culture as the ones that just left. What we know about people being "people," is that they will eventually make the same decisions as those who came before them, if subjected to the same environment (if external environmental factors are held constant).

So far, it seems that organizational memory is a combination of the strategies, polices and practices that the organization adopts as well as the collective memory of those living within the organization. There is at least one more component to organizational memory that differentiates an average organization from the truly exceptional one and that is what leads us down the Garden Path.

> *"Gardening requires lots of water—*
> *most of it in the form of perspiration."*
> *- Lou Erickson*

The best garden paths are ones that contain pleasant experiences around each gentle curve. You wander down a pleasant path, looking at plantings on both sides, and then upon rounding a bend, you find yourself in a spot that contains a unique flowering bush, a welcoming bench or an enchanting piece of art. It is even better if those experiences occur in the most unexpected places. While it might seem like an aesthetic piece of art, dependent on the skill of a talented artist, the formula for determining what makes for a pleasant garden path is a well known quantity, and it is not too difficult if you know the formula and you know how to apply it in differing circumstances (even I have been known to create an interesting pathway every now and again). The formula for knowledge capture within organizations may feel as elusive to some as the techniques for designing garden paths, but just like garden paths, it is possible to apply technique to knowledge capture as well.

Smaller, fast growing organizations tend to rely on individuals with expert information in order to accomplish their tasks. "How do you do this? So and so in department zebra knows how to do that, see them." But what happens when that person in department zebra is no longer there? That knowledge, that piece of organizational memory might be forever lost. Systematic knowledge capture and the accessibility of that knowledge to others in the organization is a critical component of organizational memory—if an organization wants to prosper and grow. It is the difference between going to the local bakery—where the proprietor can make 12 wonderful donuts at a time in one location—and rolling out a Dunkin Donuts chain worldwide.

Yet too often, this systematic collection of information also results in more mass produced, mediocre products. For the sake of expediency and often profit, the enchanting garden pathway becomes a straight concrete walkway though a grass lawn. The internal logic going on might be, "It is easier to take care of, lasts longer, costs less to build and has a host of other wonderful qualities." And consumers, both end users and business to business often look at this end state and are unhappy. How did that artesian bread that was so wonderful turn into that mass produced loaf of fluffy air with no real taste (but fortified with essential vitamins and minerals)?

Organizations have choices to make, and the hard work associated with the systematic retention and dissemination of knowledge and memories is one of those choices. As organizations grow and prosper, it is necessary for them to systematize this process if they are going to survive. However, during the systematization of the process, care must be taken not to lose sight of what made the garden pathway of interest in the first place. Your customers want to deal with an organization that seems tailored to and anticipates their individual needs. They want pleasant experiences as they round that gentle curve and set their eyes on that wonderful piece of sculpture you placed knowing they would walk down that path. Your delighted customer will come back and visit the garden often.

"Too old to plant trees for my own gratification, I shall do it for my posterity."
- Thomas Jefferson

What Would MacGyver Do?

Tuesday, May 8, 2007

Performance

There is an old folktale that describes a young man, mentioned as somewhat of a fool, who, upon getting married, was given a dowry by his father-in-law. He was told that he should become a merchant in order to provide for his new wife. Upon being swindled in his first transaction, the young man realizes that if he could read, he may be more successful as a merchant and would be less likely to be swindled in his next transaction. He heads off to the nearest large town to take reading lessons—lessons that he was told would take between six months and one year to make him proficient.

Upon entering town on the cobblestone streets, he comes across a spectacle shop in an alley. With the door to the small ancient shop open, he overhears the proprietor asking a customer as he adjusts her new glasses, "Can you read now?" The customer replies, "Yes, that is much better. I can read now." The newly wed and newly minted merchant decides he must enter the shop and ask the proprietor for glasses. For he, too, is having trouble reading. How wonderful, he thought. Rather than spending six months to one year working hard at learning how to read, all he would have to do is put on a pair of glasses!

Yet the proprietor, after giving the merchant many pairs of glasses to try on, comes to the realization that the reason his new customer can't read has nothing to do with his eyesight. Upon stating this conclusion to his customer, his customer complains that the glasses worked for the other organization...ooops! I mean "person." So why wouldn't they work for him as well?

Correct diagnosis of a situation is critical to successful problem solving implementation. What works for one organization may not work for another, and the magic silver-bullet fixes that organizations often seize upon may offer no better organizational reading ability than where they are today. While the tools of choice may vary depending on your specialty, comprehensive, customized organizational surveys have been the method of choice for me. In addition to these custom surveys, I also conduct focus groups and interviews to obtain information that is necessary for a correct diagnosis on issues surrounding organizational culture and its ability to impede or enhance performance. Sometimes, even if you correctly diagnose the situation and know what has to be done to implement change, to provide service to a customer, to help a fellow employee or maybe even save a life, often established procedures, authorizations, bureaucracy, silo thinking, inertia and organizational entropy get in the way of a successful resolution. Persistence or sometimes just flouting the system pays off—especially when you know you are right.

I know a surgeon who was describing to me a particularly tough operation he performed. He was removing part of the colon of a person with colon cancer. There is a vein that runs through the pelvis which can be cut during this procedure; upon severing this vein—just as a band under tension retracts upon being cut—it will sometimes retract into the porous surface of the pelvis, with blood upwelling from multiple small openings in the boney surface. This is a life-threatening situation, and patients have been known to bleed to death on the table when this happens. The surgeon spent a great deal of time trying to stem the flow of the blood, but clamping did not work, as there is nothing to clamp. The blood just seeps up through the bone. He tried a type of surgical epoxy glue, covering the surface of a portion of the pelvis. No success. He tried cauterization, then staples—the blood kept oozing.

He then thought of a technique that he had seen as a resident. He asked the OR staff if there were any stainless steel surgical thumbtacks available. The staff said no; the tacks were not standard equipment kept for surgical procedures. He sent people to scour the bulletin boards of the hospital to see if they held any stainless steel thumbtacks. They did and the OR staff began collecting them. As they were running them through the sterilizer, the surgeon had to get approval to use the thumbtacks in the operating room. Not standard he was told, not according to procedure. He could fill out a form and seek approval, I guess, but there were long odds against the patient living that long while forms were approved by the powers that be. A partner in the surgical practice was called upon to see a hospital administrator and explain the necessary reasons for violating established protocol.

Meanwhile, for an hour and a half, the patient lie on the table and had utilized six units of blood as the bleeding continued. Approval was given to use the thumbtacks and the surgeon pushed about 10 of them into the pelvis, in the area surrounding the upwelling blood. About 10 minutes later the bleeding stopped. The thumbtacks will be a part of this person for the rest of the patient's life, which thanks to a surgeon willing to go outside the box, will hopefully be a long one. But I bet the patient woke up with a very sore back.

This surgeon has a track record of going outside the box as evidenced by the tee shirt he received from the OR staff with, "What would MacGyver do?" emblazoned on the front. This, of course, is in reference to the popular TV show, popular a number of years ago.

The surgeon also sports another tee shirt that supports the use of duct tape for a variety of uses, but that is another story.

Correct diagnosis of issues is important to uncover—whether it is the need for glasses or a fundamental lack of reading ability, or whether it's reasons that prevent employees from getting their jobs done easily, while providing exceptional customer service or producing high quality products. Making assumptions on the causes, especially assumptions based upon what has worked or not worked elsewhere, is often misguided. Although organizations need flexibility, it is important to be innovative and to get things done in ways that are not always according to protocol—and hopefully done before the patient or organization dies.

Folktales were originally designed to teach us lessons (in addition to scaring little children), and many of their messages are still relevant today. Moreover, lessons can also be learned from an environment where most people do not expect or think that innovation is happening in real time—the operating theater. But innovation is needed in everything we do; it is how humans progress and cope with changing environmental circumstances. Lack of innovation on the correct issues will seal your fate into organizational oblivion.

We Are Currently Experiencing Unusually High Call Volumes

Wednesday, May 2, 2007

Off the Cuff

4:33 minutes and waiting. "We are currently experiencing unusually high call volumes," is a phrase that people often hear over and over again when calling a help line for a large organization. Have you ever heard, "We are experiencing call volumes as expected and have staffed appropriately, so you don't have to wait?" Or have you heard, "Our call volumes are extraordinarily low today, so you will have an unexpectedly short wait?" I don't think I ever have. Are they intentionally understaffing, but thinking that they can get away with it by putting in a soothing yet contrived "we are experiencing unusually high call volumes?" Frustrating, isn't it? How do you want your organization to be known?

10:26 minutes and waiting. Are homebuilders who advertise "bonus rooms" in houses saying that buyers do not have to pay for this space? That this "unexpected" room, this "bonus" is free? Or are they charging for it, but think that you should simply be happy about this unexpected, almost decadent space? If they are charging for it, it is not a bonus, but rather, is simply square footage that you are paying for.

15:44 minutes and waiting. Oh, you wanted the "good" engine with that car, metallic paint, you say? That will be extra. I expect that all-you-can-eat salad bars are priced for the amount of food that they would expect an average person to eat, but what would happen if you sat around all day and slowly noshed on the entire contents of the salad bar. Maybe you bring *War and Peace* with you and settle into a nice snack. Would they throw you out? I suspect they would. Want free drink refills with that salad?

20:27 minutes and waiting. One survey that was done a while back asked customers how many times a phone should ring before an operator picked it up. The customers said no more than four rings. The company came up with a novel approach in meeting that requirement. Rather than having enough operators to answer all calls by the fourth ring, the company increased the time interval between rings to give the operators more time to pick up the call.

21:30 minutes and waiting. Ever try to read the fine print on a credit card application? One professor had her class of about-to-graduate lawyers, about 30 of them, spend the entire class time trying to understand the fine print and determine what interest rate a cardholder would actually pay. They couldn't. How do you want your company to be known?

23:55 minutes and waiting. One manufacturer was concerned that the customers were complaining on a survey about product delivery times. They did not understand. They almost always got the product delivered when promised. They never asked the customer, however, when the customers needed it. They were focused on internal processes rather than on external needs.

24:30 minutes and waiting. In linkage study after linkage study, it has been shown that employee attitudes affect customer attitudes and that employee and customer attitudes have an impact on organizational performance and success, including financial performance. So why do these organizations behave the way they do? Ways that are sure to frustrate their customers? I think many of these organizations survive simply because the competition is having worse or just as bad execution problems.

25:45 minutes and got to go. Just got the operator. Anyone want to add to the list?

Feedback

Monday, April 23, 2007

Human Resources

"Performance Review May Have Sparked NASA Shooting," screams a *CNN* headline. In Houston, the local police were trying to determine a motive for why a NASA contractor fatally shot his boss and took another employee hostage before killing himself at the Johnson Space Center. It seems that this boss sent him an email performance review that was critical of his performance. Performance review by email? NASA has said that they will review security procedures. I could not help but add in my mind, "what about performance appraisal procedures?" Shouldn't those be reviewed as well? It seems like a classic case of ignoring the underlying issue. If it proves out that the performance appraisal was the key, tightening security only gives the next person who wants to smuggle in a handgun a slightly greater challenge to overcome—rather than addressing the root cause.

Not too long ago on an employee survey in which attitudinal responses could be matched up to peoples' performance appraisal ratings, we saw that the largest gap between the highest rated performers and the lowest rated performers was "feeling valued by the organization." Receiving a poor performance appraisal did not affect peoples' intention to stay or leave, their feelings about the appraisal in helping them improve their performance, or a host of other potential actions. The one thing it did affect in this organization was the self-report by poor performers that they did not feel valued. So if the goal of this performance appraisal system was to make a certain group of employees feel less valued by the organization, it was working. If the goal was something else, it was not.

In one manufacturing organization with a union, the goal (not officially stated) of the performance appraisal system was simply to document poor performance. "Write 'em up," was a commonly used expression—the thinking being that the organization needed to build a case in order to withstand the inevitable challenge from the union should it need to dismiss a person.

Meanwhile, at the Russian News Service, which controls a number of radio broadcast stations in Russia, good news is becoming official policy. *The New York Times* reported that the managers of the news service had implemented a policy, in which at least 50 percent of the news coverage on or about Russia must be positive. These apparent Kremlin allies also stated that opposition leaders could not be mentioned, and the United States was to be portrayed as an enemy. "When we talk of death, violence or poverty, for example, this is not positive," said one editor at the station. "If the stock market is up, that is positive. The weather can also be positive."

I don't know about you, but I truly do believe in the benefits that a free press brings to society; this kind of manipulation makes my skin crawl. In one fell swoop, the Russian News Service has made itself irrelevant and will now begin a decline into oblivion unless it changes course. By putting out 50 percent positive feedback as a "rule," its credibility in accurately portraying the news is zero, and the Russians—as they have done before—will turn toward external sources of news to find out what is really happening.

Are people so fragile that they can "snap" upon hearing bad performance appraisal news? Are they so easily manipulated that if you feed them a diet of pabulum that they will fall in line with official "policy," actually believing that all is well due to a steady diet of good news? Of course, the reality is likely to be where it usually resides—somewhere in the middle.

I was at a meeting recently where the facilitator put on a demonstration for the 100 or so people in the room. He told everyone to get up, walk around the room and randomly stop and describe to someone an issue you would improve upon. We were then required to the advice the person had to offer you to improve in that area. Issues were things like "listening more," or "not rushing to judgment," or "making more time for family." The person, with whom you described your issue to, was supposed to offer one thing that you could try to improve in that area—preferably something that had worked for them. Two rules: you could not interrupt your advisor, you had to just listen; second, at the end, all you were allowed to say to the person giving you advice was, "Thank you." At the end the 20 to 30 minutes, we all returned to our seats and were probed about what we thought about this performance improvement session. The results were generally very positive. What did we like about this performance appraisal session? It was non-judgmental, it was non-threatening and it was done by someone who did not have an ulterior motive or an axe to grind with you. Therefore, we could listen with an open mind and maybe get something out of the conversation. Maybe.

How many of us could say that our performance appraisal systems, which were designed to help improve the performance of the organization, are non-judgmental, non-threatening and done in a truly unbiased fashion. Anyone? It would seem that the systems we have put in place to improve performance are designed in such a fashion as to make that noble goal fairly unlikely. Can it be that performance appraisal and organizational improvement are incompatible? Anyone care to try building one again?

In survey research, I have yet to see a performance appraisal system that is well rated by the employees living under that system. Let's assume that the vast majority of people come to work wanting to do a good job. I think that is a safe assumption by the way. Therefore, if we were to create a positive working culture in the organization through tried and true principles, and people want to do a good job anyway, maybe we should scrap our performance appraisal systems and develop "organizational improvement systems."

Consequently, our conversations will be around what the individual can do to help contribute to organizational goals and what skills and abilities they need to develop to help make that happen. What about the five percent of the population that is not doing a good job and need to be eased out of the organization? I believe that their performance issues should not be addressed through the organizational improvement system, but should be addressed by a separate performance system—a system that would be irrelevant to 95 percent of the workforce.

What about organizations that tie performance appraisal to merit increase? How would this happen if there is no appraisal of someone's performance? How could we differentiate top performers who will get four to five percent increases from average performers who will get three percent? Do we really need performance appraisal systems to differentiate a one to two percentage point difference in salary increases? Seems kind of silly, doesn't it? We should be able to find a different path.

Organizations take a hit from an employee attitude standpoint when they are seen as not doing enough to correct poor employee performance. And in fact, they take even more of a hit when the organization is a unionized environment. In other words, people who are doing a good job and working hard want the others who are around them to be working hard and doing a good job as well. However, designing performance appraisal systems that are needed for five percent of the population, yet are onerous to 95 percent seems to be a monumental misjudgment.

If our goal is to create superb working environments, where people can fulfill their potential and organizations can excel at delivering products and services to their customers, we need to roll up our sleeves and get to work. We have a lot of redesigning to do.

Employee Loyalty
in an Oompa-Loompa World

Sunday, March 25, 2007

Human Resources

"While traveling abroad in search of new candy flavors, Willy Wonka encountered a race of tiny people called Oompa-Loompas. Hunted by vicious beasts such as the Snozzwangers and wicked Whangdoodles, the Oompa-Loompas had taken refuge in the tree tops of Loompaland living only on mashed green caterpillars, they desired cocoa beans above anything. Wonka immediately invited the entire Oompa-Loompa colony to his factory. Now the Oompa-Loompas comprise the entire chocolate factory workforce—in exchange for all the cocoa beans they desire."
- From Willy Wonka and the Chocolate Factory

The Oompa-Loompas in Willy Wonka and the Chocolate Factory were in a sticky situation. Their basic needs, such as safety and food, were not being met. One would suspect that the children were suffering terribly, eating only mashed green caterpillars. So Oompa-Loompas reached an agreement, a compact, with Willy Wonka. He gave them a safe place to live and all the cocoa beans they wanted, and in exchange, they provided the labor that made his chocolate factory run. For them, the bargain provided a much better environment and their loyalty to Willy was high—at least in the beginning. What hypothetically could unfold next for them? As economic conditions improved and additional opportunities for the Oompa-Loompas from other chocolate factories came about, Oompa-Loompas began to demand a livable wage and shorter workweeks. They resented the fact that Willy looked outside of the factory for a successor to himself, wondering why none of them was good enough. One was quoted as saying, "We have given our lives to making this place successful and now that Willy is thinking of retiring, he is choosing to bring in a new CEO from the outside rather than promoting from within." The Oompa-Loompas decided they needed third party representation and a general strike was called. Willy was beside himself, not understanding how those he had rescued and provided for, those he brought into his factory and treated like family, could be so ungrateful.

There has been a lot written about the changing role of organizations in terms of their responsibility to employees and, in turn, the employees' responsibilities to them. What is the current compact between employees and their employers? What do employers expect and what is foremost on the minds of today's employees? What are employees hoping to get out of an employment situation? Are there similarities to these factors as we travel the globe? Are they willing to work...for beans?

Years ago, organizations, in order to compete for talent and have a stable skilled workforce, offered what was described as cradle to grave employment—high job security, part of a paternalistic approach. Through various iterations, it is safe to say that few organizations are willing to offer that approach to employment. Yet they still desire the loyalty of the employee, convinced that having a loyal workforce is a path to organizational success. Some people I have talked to lament that "today's workers have no loyalty; they just hop from employer to employer." I strongly suspect that the reason for the lack of loyalty rests firmly in terms of how they perceive themselves being treated by the employer. Loyalty is a two-way street. How do you achieve loyalty in today's environment? What is the new compact that organizations need to forge with their workforce?

Let's examine one aspect. Some organizations have responded to the need in re-establishing loyalty by offering innovative perks such as concierge services, game rooms, onsite dry-cleaning, special prizes, killer cafeterias and a host of other convenience factors. These kinds of perks are attractive and no one is going to say, "Oh! Please, no. I just couldn't eat another free five-star meal." But I firmly believe that these organizations are all on the wrong track. These kinds of perks are really just another form of paternalism and don't get to the heart of what is important to employees long term.

Employers today should establish a compact with employees of mutuality. What is mutuality? Mutuality is when a win-win situation is created for both the firm and for the employees within the firm. For instance, one aspect of mutuality revolves around job security. Employers can no longer guarantee life-long job security and many employees no longer expect it. But an employee is likely to feel that if they can no longer be guaranteed a job here, they need to keep their eyes open, and if a better opportunity comes along, maybe they should grab it. "After all, I have no guarantees if I stick around." So how might an employer overcome a sense of temporariness that has been created?

One way would be to increase the confidence level that the firm's employees have in their ability to find another job in their field. If I am eminently employable, then the pressure to grab another job when one comes along is actually less. I can wait. While at first it may sound counter-intuitive, employers should work diligently to keep their employees' skills and education as current as possible. They should work hard to make their employees marketable and attractive to other potential employers. If employees are attractive to others, they will be more attractive to their current organization as well. Employees, seeing that the company cares enough to develop them, are more likely to stick around for further development opportunities, and this mutuality of benefit will result in an increase in employee loyalty. By keeping employees up-to-date in their skill sets, not only does the company benefit by the enhanced skill set, but it also benefits by keeping that skill set in-house. Additional benefits are likely to accrue from the extra flexibility afforded to the organization that increased education and skills of their workforce would bring about.

POINTS OF VIEW

Points of View

TUESDAY, MARCH 20, 2007

ORGANIZATIONS

> *"We have to believe in free-will. We've got no choice."*
> *- Isaac Bashevis Singer*

A family of four deer crossed in front of my car this morning. I slowed down and proceeded with caution as the road was densely forested on both sides—a straggler or two always seem to cross after you think it's safe to proceed. My daughter, riding in the back seat, offered an observation. "How come deer always wait for a car to come along before crossing the road in front of it?" Seems like a perfectly reasonable statement from a seven year old, who while precocious (of course), still struggles in seeing the world from perspectives other than her own point of view (don't we all?).

I explained that the deer cross the road when they desire and don't actually wait for a car to pass by in order to jump in front of it—it only seems that way. However, to an observer who regularly passes by in a car, who only observes the deer crossing when they drive by, it seems like a perfectly reasonable explanation that deer cross the road only upon viewing a car, which creates an uncontrollable urge on the deer's part to run in front of it.

If a tree falls in the forest and there is no one there to hear it, does it make a sound? Can a sound exist if there is no one there to hear it? If you think that existence is human centric, then the answer is not as clear as if you believe that humans are merely part of the story of what is going on around us. The tree will create the same vibration through space whether there is any measuring device—i.e., someone's ears, nearby. (We can get deeper into this, making assumptions about an event happening, but nothing, absolutely nothing—no mechanism, no organism—being there to perceive the event.)

It also reminds me of Schrödinger's Cat—an example used to illustrate the point in the world of quantum mechanics—that has a cat in a box. Upon opening the box to examine the state of the cat (alive or dead), you actually change the state of the cat. In other words, the very act of measuring something can cause its properties to change.

For the purists in the survey world, we could argue that when you ask people about "overall satisfaction with their organization," you run the risk of actually changing the way that they could respond. This might be especially true if you first ask about other aspects of organizational life, which can get them thinking about issues that they had not been previously thinking about. On the other hand, the pragmatist in me says that if you ask the question routinely in the same fashion, at the same point in the questionnaire, it is not a big issue. Work done on item placement on surveys shows that it can have an impact—but rather minimal in my opinion—when you are looking for big organizational elephants to tackle rather than nuanced differences.

What about other aspects of life, organizational or otherwise? Do we routinely use the same causality logic that is driven from the point of view of the observer, as when deer cross the road? I have an inkling that many of us do, even when we know better. I am pretty sure, for instance, that the road repair crews have discussions to determine which way I will be driving that day before setting out the cones and construction equipment. I am also sure that upon seeing me get into their line, tollbooth operators and parking lot attendants decide to slow down the flow of cars in my lane. And I am 100 percent certain that if there are multiple lines at a highway exit, ticket window or at airport security that the longest, slowest moving line is the one I am supposed to be in. By this point, I have just given up, and now automatically move toward that line. (That last one may have a basis in reality, if you think about normal distributions and the likelihood that you need to go where the majority of other people need to go).

Upon starting work with a new client, a client that I may never have previously known much about or thought of, I start to see its logos and products everywhere I look. The organization is more cognizant to me personally rather than actually having more advertising, products or services out there.

Does the observer's point-of-view influence his or her interpretation of events? Of course it does. High-ranking managers, especially in larger organizations, may not get the opportunity to observe organizational events the same way as others in the organization experience them. They tend to be shielded from this (if you were cynical, you would say that they are being managed by their subordinates), which may cause them to conclude that their organization is running in a fashion incongruent with reality.

One reason why organizational surveys are as popular as they have been over the years is because they can help cut through the shielding. Senior management is often captivated during a feedback session because it offers a point of view that may be rare for them to experience.

The notion of free will revolves around the concept of whether people (and deer) have freedom of choice in choosing which decisions they will make, or whether our outcomes, our fates have been predetermined by some external force. However, the choices we make are inextricably bound up with our interpretations of events— our point of view. The implementation of free will is then potentially also driven by the fact that two people who observe the same event may interpret the event differently. Consequently, these individuals may take different courses of action, depending on their point of view, which varies their interpretation of the event. A single interpretation of an event is not likely from all observers because of the unique point of view of the various observers. All you have to do is to listen to the various "news" shows that are popular today to realize how varied the "neutral" interpretation of events can be.

People within organizations, and those helping them interpret events and other data flows that impinge upon the organization, face a challenge. In order to make the best possible decisions for the organization, the challenge is to examine openly events from multiple points of view and to come to the realization that decisions made will be interpreted differently depending on the point of view of the observer. You may come to what you view as the optimum decision, but realize it will be interpreted divergently. Therefore, you will need additional explanation and transparency to be understandable from the viewpoint of others. Wait…I think I just saw a deer cross the road.

Surrogate Measures

Sunday, March 11, 2007

Employee Research

We are surrounded by surrogate measures; they exist everywhere in life. A surrogate measure is when a particular measurable or observable condition is assumed meaningful about an underlying state or condition. They are usually used when it is difficult, impossible or unknown how to measure the underlying condition directly.

For example, last summer we had the first tornado in Westchester County in 30 years. There was much debate regarding whether there was a tornado. If it was, how strong was it? Was it rated on the Fujita scale? A tornado expert from NOAA showed up and determed whether cars had been picked up, roofs had been torn off and trees had a twisting pattern around their breaks. He then pronounced that we had a strong F1 or a weak F2 tornado. All of these signs of damage are surrogate ways of measuring whether there was a tornado and what its wind speed was.

When a car is involved in a serious accident, the police are very busy afterward, taking measurements of skid marks and other signs of speed, investigating failure to yield and looking for other indicators of what happened. All of these measures are surrogate measures of what actually happened because there are no printouts yet available from cars regarding "black box" measures—measures that are available in airplanes after an accident, logging the actual conditions that led to the accident. These measures are made in order to make assumptions about specific accident conditions.

Surrogate measures abound in the medical world with doctors examining patients for all kinds of signs of underlying medical conditions that are not directly observable. These initial signs may lead to more involved tests, which may be more evolved or advanced surrogate measures to help further define patient ills. Unfortunately, sometimes the actual extent of the illness cannot be determined until the surgeon begins cutting, or a biopsy of the tissue itself is done. The fact that autopsies are still regularly performed indicates the limits of surrogate measures in medical diagnosis.

A subset of surrogate measures that has always intrigued me is called unobtrusive measures. When surrogate measures are used to make assumptions about an underlying condition in a manner where people affected may not even realize that they are being measured, the measurements are called unobtrusive. An example would be looking at the wear and tear of floors in museums to determine the popularity of exhibits. The assumption being made that those exhibits surrounded by excessive wear and tear are more popular then those holding up well (as opposed to the possibility of poor quality flooring in front of those exhibits).

An entire set of potentially bias-related surrogate measures are used when we observe people—their appearance, their dress, hair length, skin color, age and gender—to make assumptions regarding their beliefs, expected behaviors or capabilities. These types of surrogate measures, which can be quite poorly correlated to the reality of beliefs and behaviors, will often lead to inaccurate conclusions and come about because of a tendency of people to quickly categorize others—often inappropriately.

Organizations and organizational psychologists use a whole host of surrogate measures in determining or making assumptions about underlying conditions in organizations and for use in employee selection. Surveys of organizational attributes are measuring those attributes using a series of surrogate measures. When we ask people if they have the training they need to do their jobs, we surmise that if they answer affirmatively, these employees will be capable of better job performance than individuals responding in the negative will. Some of the questions used in organizational surveys are better surrogate measures than others, and it is the role of the survey expert to write questionnaires that use the best measures possible—those surrogates that are better indicators of actual or potential organizational performance. Indices tied to constructs (e.g. loyalty and engagement) are simply average of surrogates or construct surrogates.

Let's take a step back for a minute and ask ourselves why are we doing organizational surveys in the first place? In my opinion, the whole purpose of conducting organizational surveys is to help improve organizational performance—the effectiveness and efficiency of the organization. Many make the assumption, as do I, that having an environment that is perceived positively by the workforce and that has certain attributes can help organizations perform. The survey itself then is a set of surrogate measures asking people about the characteristics of the organizational environment.

A well-done organizational survey uses the best possible surrogate measures to make assumptions about the actual conditions within the organizational environment—those conditions that have been demonstrated to be linked to important organizational outcomes. Surrogate measures within many fields have evolved over time with more predictive surrogates, which are better measures of underlying conditions replacing less informative ones. It is the role and responsibility of organizational psychologists and other survey experts to push the field by continuing to search for better surrogate measures that help those who entrust us with consulting for their organizations.

A Lesson Never Learned

Sunday, March 18, 2007

Around the World

> *"Now, I say to you today my friends, even though we face the difficulties*
> *of today and tomorrow, I still have a dream. It is a dream deeply*
> *rooted in the American dream. I have a dream that one day this nation*
> *will rise up and live out the true meaning of its creed: 'We hold these*
> *truths to be self-evident, that all men are created equal.'"*
> *- Martin Luther King, Jr., August 28, 1963*

Phillip Zimbardo did some of the most interesting, depressing work ever done by a psychologist. He showed just how easily one person or group can dehumanize another. His experiment was called the Prison Experiment, and was conducted at Stanford in 1971. In this experiment, a group of college student volunteers randomly split into two groups. One group became "prisoners," and the other became "guards." After a short period of time, drastic changes in behavior began to occur due to the situation the "guards" and "prisoners" found themselves in—behavior that demonstrated situational cues, rather than actual differences in people, caused one group to behave cruelly to another.

In fact, the situation became so dire that the experiment was ended ahead of schedule. From Dr. Zimbardo's website: "At this point it became clear that we had to end the study. We had created an over-whelmingly powerful situation—a situation in which prisoners were withdrawing and behaving in pathological ways, and in which some of the guards were behaving sadistically. Even the "good" guards felt helpless to intervene, and none of the guards quit while the study was in progress....And so, after only six days, our planned two-week prison simulation was called off."

This experiment sadly demonstrated how badly people could behave toward others, using situational cues, peer pressure and expectations to drive their behavior—cues that often have nothing to do with the persons themselves. This pattern of dehumanizing behavior has occurred repeatedly throughout human history and is sadly, certainly to be repeated once again in the future.

Africa, the birthplace of humanity, has certainly seen its share of suffering and inhumanity over the ages. It is both very poor and very rich at the same time. Very poor in terms of how groups treat each other, leading to some extremely violent, really terrible behavior; very poor in its history of human rights, in its legendary corruption and constant vying for power by some dictator or another; and for some reason, very poor in the willingness of the world to lend a hand in a way that can make a lasting difference. Africa is rich in mineral, timber and oil resources, so it was only a matter of time until China, with its growing thirst for resources, cast an eye towards Africa. When I first read about this, I have to admit feeling a ray of hope. Maybe the Chinese can succeed where everyone else has failed. Maybe the Chinese can help lift the continent of Africa out of the pattern of almost perpetual bad news. The Chinese were able to turn a huge country that was essentially poverty stricken into a growing economic juggernaut. Could some of what China learned work in Africa?

For a long time, China had been among the world's "have nots"—taken advantage of and looked down upon by others. In one instance, the opium wars were fought to ensure the British right to import opium into China. The opium trade in China had very serious, negative consequences on individual health and the economic health of China, consequences that the British chose to ignore, as that country's main concern was balancing its trade deficit. The Japanese, during World War II, treated the Chinese very poorly (as well as a host of others), looking down upon them as somehow something less than human. In Nanjing, China, the Japanese army killed an estimated 300,000 civilians and POWs, and raped at least 20,000 women during a two-month period. The means used to kill these people is almost beyond description. There is virtually no country in the world, some to a lesser extent and some to a greater extent, which does not have versions of these sordid acts in their own history—including the U.S. The point is not to single out any one country, but to paint a general pattern that describes how humankind can be inhuman to humankind.

China is now rapidly becoming one of the world's "haves." And given its history and the trauma that the Chinese have suffered over the years, would it be possible that the Chinese would take a fresh approach in their dealings with Africa and other "have nots?" Can they break the mold of "situational judgment," whereby certain characteristics are ascribed to people because of the environment they are in and not who they really are? Has the country's own personal experiences prepared the Chinese to interact in a more positive fashion with today's "have nots?" The verdict is still out, but there are some troubling signs emerging.

Appearing in the International Herald Tribune (February 17, 2007) is this excerpt from the opinion page:

> *China's president, Hu Jintao, recently completed a 12-day, 8-nation African tour in which he dispensed billions of dollars' worth of debt relief, discounted loans and new investments....Beijing's huge purchases of oil and other re-*

sources have made it the continent's third-largest trading partner...China's oil appetite has drawn it into an ugly partnership with Sudan, which is waging a genocidal war in Darfur that has already killed at least 200,000 people.

Chinese mining investors in Zambia, as focused on the bottom line as any capitalists, have drawn complaints from workers and environmentally minded neighbors. China's lending banks do not subscribe to the international guidelines, known as the Equator Principles, which are used to monitor and manage the social and environmental impact of major outside investments. And a flood of cheap Chinese manufactured goods has pushed some of the poorest and most marginal workers deeper into poverty and unemployment...China isn't the first outside industrial power to behave badly in Africa. But it should not be proud of following the West's sorry historical example.

And appearing on the on the cover of *The Wall Street Journal* (February 2, 2007) is the story of Chambishi, Zambia:

Set amid rolling hills in Zambia's copper belt, Chambishi was supposed to be a showcase of Sino-African friendship. China's state metals conglomerate...bought the mothballed copper mine here in 1998, bringing plenty of jobs and investments. Initial gratitude, however, quickly turned into seething discontent, as the new Chinese owners banned union activity and cut corners on safety. In 2005, dozens of locals were killed in a blast at the Chinese explosives facility serving the mine—the worst industrial accident in Zambia's history. Then, the following year, protesting Zambian employees were sprayed with gunfire. 'The Chinese, they don't even consider us to be human beings...They think they have the right to rule us,' says a former miner who says he was shot by a Chinese supervisor.

Sometimes extreme events accentuate behavior patterns and can serve as a magnifier of experiences we have in our day-to-day lives. Lessons learned from extreme events can bring clarity to how more common situations can be successfully worked through. For instance, people face traumas as organizations merge, acquire, downsize and reorganize. Some organizations do a much better job than others in dealing with these traumas and the employees' associated stress. These organizational traumas are no different from larger traumas that people would experience when facing the death of a spouse, child or parent, or living through a terrorist attack—the degree of the trauma is the difference. Larger traumas can magnify human reactions and allow us to see more clearly our needs and shortcomings.

Some organizations over the years have created "classes" of people that are somehow looked down upon, not part of the team. In organizations with poor labor/management relations, militant unions can arise. What is management's typical response to the rise of unions? Will they look inward and wonder, "What have we done that has created conditions where our employees (often called our most valuable asset) felt the need to form or join a union?" And how can we correct this situation? Some management respond appropriately; others will seek to dehumanize the employees and the unions, just as the "guards" in Phil Zimbardo's experiment did to the "prisoners."

A case in point comes from a story appearing in *The Wall Street Journal* (February 9th, 2007), about the U.S. Air Marshall Service. After 9/11, the Service greatly expanded, but grueling schedules, lack of advancement, onerous rules affecting individuals' abilities to perform their jobs and lack of identity protection have resulted in "many" (in the words of other Marshalls) quitting the Service. What was the response from the head of the Service? He called the complainers "disgruntled amateurs, insurgents, and organizational terrorists." What about the response of the Marshalls? They joined a union. Luckily, there is now a new head of the U.S. Air Marshall Service. Interestingly, within its own borders, China is passing laws that give greater protection to workers and increasing authority to unions. The enforcement of those laws is still questionable. The Chinese Embassy in the U.S. cites a report to the Chinese government that documented worker abuses:

- According to the results of a survey, in 2000, 36.6 billion yuan worth of wages was delayed (4.4 billion U.S. dollars) for urban workers by employers across China. This figure may exceed 40 billion yuan to date.

- For migrant workers, mostly poor farmers, the situation is even worse. Experts put the delayed payment of wages for them at 100 billion yuan annually, and it is common for them to get no additional pay for overtime.

- Workshop safety remains a problem for many workers, mostly those working for private or overseas-funded plants. In Leqing city of Zhejiang Province, East China, trade union officials said about 5,000 migrant workers lost some of their fingers last year while working at poor quality punches without safety devices. Those injured were kicked out of the plants by their bosses with little financial compensation, which is against the law, union officials said.

This description of the U.S. Air Marshall Service, the state of labor relations within China and China's behavior in Africa are simply severe, magnified descriptions of what happens within our own organizations on a routine basis. Organizations are made up of humans—humans who are subject to all of our nobility, all of our frailty and all of our shortcomings. Can we learn from Phil Zimbardo and make our organizations truly better places to inhabit? Will this lesson of dehumanizing those who are different from us, those who based on economic conditions find themselves with fewer options teach us anything? Can we evolve into something more than we are today? On good days, when I read about some of the truly inspiring efforts that people do to help others, I am filled with hope. Other times, when I read a story of a supervisor shooting an employee to keep the others in line, or of a factory throwing out employees who lost their fingers while working as though they were damaged goods, I'm filled with sorrow.

> *"I am somehow less interested in the weight and convolutions of Einstein's brain than in the near certainty that people of equal talent have lived and died in cotton fields and sweatshops."*
> *- Stephen Jay Gould*

Virtuous And Deleterious Cycles

Sunday, March 4, 2007

Organizations

Here in the Northeast, the sap is running, and sugaring operations are underway. Maple tree farmers have inserted their taps and are collecting the sap from the Sugar Maple trees, which will be condensed into that golden amber color that we all so love on our breakfast treats. For me, it is the ultimate signal that spring is just around the corner and a harbinger that I will soon be able to get out into the garden and begin planting for the new season—the beginning of a new cycle.

An article in the local paper last week described how the Sugar Maples might be threatened due to climatic changes; it may become too warm for them to survive in their current locations. While the trees might perish in their current locations, the Sugar Maple may be able to retreat across our northern border to Canada in order to survive as a species and to hopefully maintain sugaring as an industry.

A common question that I get about employee survey results in organizations revolves around the chicken and the egg question—another kind of cycle. The questions generally goes something like this: "Do you get positive survey results because the business performance is good, or does good business performance lead to good survey results?" Ah, causality. It can be a very difficult question to answer, but in many respects, it is the wrong question. Correlations, regressions and other commonly used techniques to analyze employee survey responses simply describe the current state of affairs and do not indicate causality. Without true experimental design, which is very rare in this kind of fieldwork, causality is at best based on assumptions.

It is certainly true that in highly performing organizations that generate large profit, it is easier to do things, like providing sizable raises, bonuses, great heath care or other opportunities that will impact employees' perceptions about the place. It's about being part of a "winning team," but how did that "winning team" get attracted to and begin performing at the level necessary to allow the organization to become highly performing in the first place? Rather than debating that chicken or egg argument, suffice it to say, organizations that can get on this "virtuous cycle," a self-perpetuating cycle of higher performance, will outperform those that are caught up in a "deleterious cycle," a downward spiral of performance.

So it isn't the debate itself that is important; in fact, the debate itself is a waste of energy and time. What is important is to get onto that virtuous cycle. There is not one assured way of doing this, but by looking at organizations that seem to be on those cycles, a pattern emerges—a pattern that it would behoove others to emulate. Organizations that are on virtuous cycles can be described as having some combination of the following: a brand that others aspire to, a brand that attracts other high quality workers, high quality products, dominant market share, paradigm changing innovations; a workforce that feels clear on what the organization is about and its role in it, a workforce that is given the tools and resources it needs to deliver on organizational goals and a workforce that feels equitably treated given what it puts into the organization; and employees that have a positive, fulfilling future should they stick around with the organization.

Do you create the business performance or the environment that nurtures it first? The answer is both. One does not cause the other;

one is not a precursor to the other, but rather putting both of these aspects into place creates the environment that allows organizations to get on the virtuous cycle.

Deleterious cycles can kick in at any time in organizational life as well, and they need to be scrupulously guarded against. I remember hiring a PR firm a number of years ago that charged what I thought was an outrageously high amount for helping my company gain publicity in relevant industry and general publications. After about a one-year period, I expressed my displeasure with its performance. The firm, of course, felt it was being fairly compensated for the work, but suggested that if I was not happy with its performance that I could be charged less per month—and although unstated—do a bit less. Rather than accept this, I viewed this as a downward or deleterious cycle. I would pay less because I was unhappy. But I was not unhappy about the amount, I was unhappy about what I was getting for the amount. And because I was paying less, I would get less performance, which would likely result in even less success in terms of getting the company into the relevant press. I changed to a different PR firm rather than begin that downward spiral.

Another type of "self-correcting" deleterious cycle can be described by looking at tax codes in developed countries. Over a period of time, the tax legislation becomes more and more complex with the only beneficiaries being the tax accountants and lawyers who charge more for completing increasingly more complex tax forms. One reaction to these increasingly burdensome tax laws and rates is to look for places where some relief can be obtained. The Economist, in a recent edition, describes one benefit of tax havens, those small off-shore locations where people and organizations can shelter income, as a correcting mechanism for getting countries off the deleterious cycle of increasingly onerous tax legislation. The publication states that when a country feels enough pain from these tax shelters, it will cause the nation to examine and potentially spur overhauls to its tax codes. (Or is that wishful thinking?) This describes how an external influence, tax havens, becomes a key to getting an organization (a country in this case) off a deleterious cycle—should they choose to take advantage of it. Similar kinds of pressures, correction mechanisms, were previously felt by the automotive industry as the Japanese developed higher quality and better cars than Detroit. These external influencers, which can be viewed as potentially beneficial, are seen in numerous kinds of situations.

What is interesting now is that organizations in the era of globalization are able to take advantage of others' virtuous cycles, instead of simply adapting to outside pressures to correct deleterious cycles in their own performance. Outsourcing or off shoring are potential examples of this. An organization that has difficultly dealing with manufacturing internally could simply outsource its internal problem (whether it is cost or quality or speed) to someone perceived as more capable. But it leaves one wondering, if organizations are taking advantage of the virtuous cycles to be found elsewhere, does that mean that they feel less pressure to correct fundamental deleterious cycles that exist internally? Is it a way to avoid dealing with some problems or is this simply a new way of doing business?

Is Grandpa Going To Be Okay?

Tuesday, February 6, 2007

PERFORMANCE

I was in the car driving home from Grandma and Grandpa's house with my wife and daughter in the back seat. My seven-year old daughter asked in a worried voice whether Grandpa was going to be okay. My wife responded that she did not know, that we all hoped so and that everything was being done to try to ensure the reoccurrence of his cancer would be brought back under control. My daughter demanded again, "Do you think he will be okay?" When my wife said she did not know, my daughter said, "Guess." Then she asked again, "Do you think he will be okay?" Again, my wife replied in a soothing way about how everyone— all the doctors and each of us—were trying to make sure he got better, but that she did not know. My daughter said once more, "Guess." How she longed to hear the words from us that Grandpa will be okay, that we could make everything all right. She then wanted to go back to their house so she could be with him, as though spending time with him could wish him back to health. Unfortunately, wishing does not necessarily make it so—not even when you really want it to.

Wishing sometimes seems to have an impact in our lives—at least we hope that it does. Benedict Carey, writing in *The New York Times* (January 13, 2007), describes in an article titled, "Do You Believe In Magic" recent research that looks at the origins of superstitions and belief in magical powers. We have known for a very long time that people have superstitious beliefs, that certain behaviors are thought to lead to desired outcomes, whether that be as simple as wearing "my lucky shirt" to a ball game or other more complex beliefs. And other work clearly shows that these behaviors are not limited to human beings. What caught my eye in the article was some work that seems to point in the direction that the brain may be hardwired for a tendency toward superstitious behavior. *"The appetite for such beliefs appears to be rooted in the circuitry of the brain, and for good reason. The sense of having special powers buoys people in threatening situations, and helps soothe everyday fears and ward off mental distress. In excess it can lead to compulsive or delusional behavior."*

How many of the world's great tragedies were somehow affected by magical or wishful thinking? Was Chamberlin engaging in magical thinking when he thought that appeasement could bring peace? Could he wish it so or was this just poor judgment? Were the millions who were slaughtered in WWII engaged in magical thinking, hoping that the obvious was somehow not real or not going to happen to them? Or maybe it just became unobvious? Was it obvious only in hindsight? Are we waiting for something magical to happen in Darfur, hoping somehow, someone will have a change of heart and this current slaughter will go away? Which other of today's crises are being affected by a natural tendency of people to engage in this magical or wishful thinking?

Magical thinking and superstitious behavior can raise its head in the workplace as well and sometimes in very harmful ways. This would be especially true should additional work conclusively prove that our brains have developed this belief as a defense mechanism—a defense mechanism that does not simply shut itself off after millions of years of evolution simply because we have decided recently to take up employment and sit in desk chairs rather than on the savannah. Our evolution, our brains go with us wherever we go. What are the implications for this within the workplace?

How many people sit there wishing for a larger raise than what they are actually going to get? Or for recognition that is simply not coming? Or that with the coming reorganization, they will end up with that really great boss, or be given that position they desire? Do people sometimes not see the writing on the wall, hoping for a more favorable outcome than is maybe possible? Do they wish that under extreme circumstances somehow a white knight will come along and rescue them from a negative situation? Do they feel that if they wish for it hard enough, it will come true? Is grass really greener on the other side (inside that other company) or are we just wishing that it is so, only to find our wishful thinking to be just that—wishful. The grass only gets so green.

Making the assumption that magical or wishful thinking is detrimental to an organization's performance, transparency, clarity of decision making and communications would seem to be key within the workplace toward the reduction of certain kinds of magical thinking. A thorough understanding of an organization's culture and that culture's impact on performance, as well as the natural tendencies of people residing within the organization, would seem to be beneficial to have in hand. But magical thinking is something that is not just going to go away. It is built into us, and what we need to do is to recognize our tendencies and learn how to cope positively with them.

I, for one, have no desire for it to go away, as I am wishing really hard that Grandpa gets better and maybe if I wish hard enough...

(Grandpa is a fighter, and I have every expectation that with the rigorous medical treatments he is receiving that he will beat this—once again.)

What If Your Child Is Below Average In English?

D+

Sunday, February 18, 2007

Performance

A question was posed to me the other day. What if your child was really good in math, but below average in English? In a world of limited resources and time, should you work to improve your child's English abilities? Or should you pour your resources into an area where your child has the potential really to be a superstar? In other words, do you give up on the English and concentrate on math, or do you forego a shot at becoming a math superstar to spend some time and resources on English?

As a parent, the answer that comes to mind is that you do both. We have unconditional loyalty to our children, so you figure out a way to make both of them happen. You bring English up to an acceptable level and you work on providing whatever edge you can in math. Let's not allow that easy answer, however, and say that doing both is not possible. What do you do?

What if your child was an employee, an employee who was really good in one area, but sorely lacking in another? Is your loyalty in this case unconditional? Where do you put your effort now?

What if the choice was between two customers? One customer is average in his or her satisfaction with your services, while the other customer is dissatisfied. If you have to make a hard choice due to limited resources, is it more beneficial to an organization to resolve the dissatisfied customer's complaints or should you concentrate on making the average customer absolutely thrilled? How do you create a loyal customer?

Where do you get the biggest payback for your expenditure of resources, time and effort? Is it always a matter of payback? These are questions that people within organizations struggle with every day.

In the area of customer research, I have seen some data that suggests that thrilled customers are at least three times more likely to repurchase your product, willing to spend 10 percent more for perceived benefits and are much more likely to recommend your product or service to others. This data also indicates that dissatisfied customers are already lost, that they are typically already actively looking for alternatives to your product or service. So the case here was made that taking an average customer and making them thrilled has more benefit to the organization. How did the dissatisfied customer get that way in the first place? Are there systemic issues within the organization that will raise their heads again and affect your now thrilled customer? Without that kind of root cause examination, you may be diligently working, utilizing wishful thinking as a way to thrill your customers. Just to make matters more complicated, I recently attended a meeting where an expert on customer research suggested that this pattern varies by industry! Ah, the world is never simple, and just when I thought that a categorization was possible to simplify my thinking process, it turns out to be complicated.

What are we to do with an employee who excels in one area, but may be sorely lacking in another? Here again, the answer is more complicated than it may first appear. There are certain areas that are zero tolerance in my mind. Anything less than a high level of performance should be unacceptable. These are areas like working safely, sexual harassment and ethics. Let's put those zero tolerance issues aside for a moment. I have never seen a job performed absolutely identically by two different people. Each person has unique strengths and abilities; individuals tend to make jobs their own by bringing to bear that uniqueness. I believe that an organization is stronger when it can take advantage of those unique strengths—that potential diversity—rather than attempting to force everyone into the same mold. Saying this, there are some issues that need to be performed at a minimally acceptable level across the board, and effort needs to be expended to bring an employee up to that level. If an employee cannot achieve that level, they may not be a close enough fit to stay in the organization. Is loyalty to an employee unconditional? No, it is not, but neither should employees be treated like disposal or fungible assets or be moved around as needed like pieces on a chessboard.

What was my answer to the original question? What if your child was really good in math, but below average in English? I said that you do both. Improve the English up to a minimally acceptable level, and give them the edge that may make them a mathematical superstar. Now I am left wondering if this should always be the case (for your child, employee or customer) even when it appears not to be an option.

Mithridatism

Monday, September 3, 2007

Around the World

Slowly, over a period of time, it is possible for individuals to build a sense of complacency with the status quo, to accept organizational processes and procedures as they are, to not push the envelope, as it needs to be pushed for progress that keeps the organization sharp. We do things a certain way because that is they way we have done it in the past; it is comfortable and we know it works. There is less risk in this. Or is there?

There is a well-documented, innate tendency on the part of humans to seek consistency. Organizations receive many benefits when they're able to provide a consistent environment for their employees and consistent products for their customers. Consistency though is not complacency. Consistency is being able to perform in a similar fashion on whatever your process or products happen to be, while complacency is being satisfied with the current state of your process or products. Consistency is good, complacency is bad.

The innate tendency toward consistency can lead to complacency with the status quo. The organization and the people within it strive for consistency (to the benefit of the customers), which is much more difficult to achieve in an organization that is constantly changing. So if we don't change things, it is easier to be consistent, pleasing both customers and employees, but risking being lulled into complacency. The best organizations are those that can become rapidly consistent around delivering new products and implementing new procedures.

Complacency with the status quo can be considered a poison, slowly eating away at what made the organization come into being and achieve success in the first place. Entrenched complacency with the status quo in any organization is the end of its existence. Other new organizations that are not tied to the past, that are not burdened by legacy systems or processes will come along and surpass the complacent—sometimes slowly and sometimes not so slowly, making them obsolete. Some organizations are shaken out of their complacency and can rebound with a reinvigorated spirit, others simply fade away.

Mithridatism is the slow ingestion of non-lethal amounts of a poison over an extended period of time in order to build tolerance or partial immunity against the poison. The word has it origins from Mithridates VI, the King of Pontus (from a small area on the Black Sea that is now part of Turkey) who was so consumed with the notion that someone was trying to poison him so he regularly ingested small doses of poison. Legend has it that assassins used the technique so they could have a meal with their intended victim and suffer no ill effects while the victim fell dead from the poisoned meal. Today, some who handle poisonous snakes for a living practice this in an attempt to build up immunity in case they are accidentally bitten (Please do not try this at home).

Standards of performance evolve and change. Product quality standards and process standards need to change within organizations if they are to remain competitive and keep their customers. How do you determine and at what level do you set your operational standards?

The recent tragic collapse of the coalmine in Crandall Canyon, Utah, with six miners still missing and the deaths of several rescuers in a subsequent collapse, brought renewed focus on the issues surrounding how dangerous mining is as an occupation. And even though the standard for mine safety is set at zero accidents, each year there are deaths.

There are the aspirational standards (zero accidents), and then there are the real operational standards (procedures) that lead to specific outcomes. Aspirational standards mean nothing unless the operational standards in place are aligned with them and supported by them. Would it be possible to set new operational standards, standards that would allow a mine to operate with zero deaths? Yes, it would. But the current costs of doing so would likely mean that no mining would be done in this country and the jobs that go along with it would disappear. Right or wrong, there is tolerance on the part of the employees to accept a certain level of danger in order to be employed, on the part of the mining company to maximize its profits and on the part of our society as a whole in order to obtain cheaper goods. We have to question though whether we have become complacent with operational standards for how mines operate—the slow ingestion of a poison that in this case leads not to immunity, but to death.

In the U.S. in 2006, the death toll from mining was 72. Contrast that to China where in 2006 the death toll from mining was 4,746 (reported). However, in the early part of the 20th century the number of deaths in the U.S. from mining accidents was approximately 1,000 per year. Does this mean we cut China some slack, or do we hold it to a higher standard than the United States held itself as it industrialized? Do we have any right to hold China to a higher standard? The only justification for holding developing countries to a higher standard is globalization—a factor that did not exist in the early 20th century. Why? It is due to the new interdependencies that exist within a global marketplace and what can happen to everyone if a major component of that global marketplace collapses.

Jared Diamond, in his book *Collapse: How Societies Choose to Fail or Succeed,* examines why various societies over the millennia collapsed, with their people at best a mere memory in the historical record. Diamond lists eight historical factors and four new factors that have and may contribute to the collapse of societies:

1. Historical
   a. Deforestation and habitat destruction
   b. Soil problems (erosion, salinization and soil fertility losses)
   c. Water management problems
   d. Overhunting
   e. Overfishing
   f. Effects of introduced species on native species
   g. Human population growth
   h. Increased per capita impact of people

2. New
   a. Human-caused climate change
   b. Buildup of toxic chemicals in the environment
   c. Energy shortages
   d. Full human utilization of the Earth's photosynthetic capacity

The chief difference between what has happened to past collapsed societies and today's society is that the elements Diamond lists are now occurring on a global basis rather than in a single society. The ominous foreshadowing that occurs in the book is how similar we, as a global community, are to those societies that have disappeared. And the solutions that need to be applied to prevent a potential pending catastrophe should be applied on a global basis.

It might be a pipedream for now, but the adoption of global standards in how goods and services are produced and delivered may be what is required to prevent our global impending collapse if the storyline in the book were to play out. If we continue the storyline as it is described, will the collapse happen in 50 years, 100 years or 1,000? It is hard to say, but as a species, can we afford to be so shortsighted that we take that risk? Should we be complacent? Should goods and services, and the production of those goods and services meet a common worldwide standard that certifies them as compliant, not from simply a quality standpoint, but from a societal standpoint? Certifying that the impact that the production has on our shared global environment and on those who produced them was done in a sustainable fashion and without a variety of forms of labor abuse? Is that a new ISO certification?

The Kyoto Protocol split the world into Annex I countries (the developed world) and Non-Annex I countries (developing countries). Annex I countries, participating in the Protocol, have accepted greenhouse gas emission reductions to five percent below their 1990 levels, collectively. Non-Annex I countries do not have emission limits. Some in the United States currently believe that by requiring a reduction of greenhouse gases that we will hurt the economy—and by extension the world's economy—while some of the fastest growing economies, rapidly becoming the most polluting would be under no such restrictions.

Developing countries argue that the developed world had its opportunity to grow without restrictions that allowed them to become the economic powerhouses that they are today. And that their citizens (of the developing countries) have a right to a better life, similar to one enjoyed by others. Some of the developed countries (e.g. U.S.), argue that signing onto the Protocol would spell economic disaster and would give others an unfair advantage. They are all being shortsighted. Given the vastly greater interlocking nature of the world today, the mutual interdependencies and the likelihood that if we go down as a global society, we will all go down together, I argue that we need to hold China, the others in the developing world and the companies operating there (including mining) to a higher standard than we held ourselves as we developed. We also need to hold ourselves to an even higher standard—a much higher standard. Why? Because we need to lead by example, not to be dragged kicking and screaming into doing what is right for society from a global perspective. If America wants to preserve its current preeminent status as the world's only true superpower and not take the path of other empires that have preceded us, we need to be in the forefront of issues of world import. Yes, America is an empire (seemingly a reluctant empire), and yes, we do have unparalleled and unchallengeable military supremacy if we choose to use it; however, our real power and legitimacy comes from the economic prosperity we spread and the standards of behavior we, as a nation and as a people, employ.

In the past, wars were often the causes of technological leaps, change and growth. Many technological and medical advances came out of the necessity generated from a war environment and the corresponding flow of funding. Space exploration has also been a source of similar advancement. As a global society, we have a new war to fight, one that many do not yet see and a war upon which the future of the entire planet may ride. That war is one of developing unparalleled global prosperity as broadly as possible in such a fashion that the world itself can sustain all of us. There is only one country in the world that can lead that war today, and that is the United States of America. Our nation must step up, rally the rest of the world to fight this battle with us and assume a leadership role to make sure that we as a global society survive. Great things lie ahead for those who engage with us in winning this battle.

The flip side of this argument is that there have been numerous doomsayers over the years, concerned about the manner of all sorts of things. The world will run out of food, a global pandemic will occur, a nuclear war will make the world uninhabitable, Yellowstone will erupt once again, a neighboring star will go supernova, wiping us out in less than an eye blink, or an unexpected asteroid will do the job. Critics point out that all of these doomsday prophecies have proven to be false alarms in the past. Of course, they have been because we are still here. But that doesn't mean that we should ignore the potential and not do our best to prevent potential catastrophes because we haven't yet experienced one—that would be complacency.

Can we be complacent about what may be happening to our planet? Can organizations, whether they are companies or countries, push themselves to think outside of the box? To try a new approach, a new way of thinking about this interconnected world in which we now live? I am up for it, how about you?

The story of King Mithridates VI of Pontus does not have a happy ending. His gambit to protect himself from poisoning had an unintended consequence. He lost a war and his kingdom to Pompey (a Roman general) and tried to commit suicide by ingesting poison. Because of his acquired immunity, the poison did not work and the fallen King had to have a mercenary run him through with his sword. Mithridatism, when applied, has a very narrow application. You may develop some immunity to one specific poison, but there are innumerable other poisons and complacencies that can do you or your company in.

About the Author

JEFFREY M. SALTZMAN, M.A.

Jeffrey M. Saltzman, M.A., is the New York practice leader at Kenexa. With more than 25 years of consulting experience, he has conducted extensive employee research in diverse settings including heavy industry and high technology manufacturing, service organizations and federal government agencies. Mr. Saltzman is a regular university lecturer and is a noted conference speaker. He holds a Master of Arts degree in Industrial and Organizational Psychology from the University of Akron and a Bachelor of Arts degree from the State University of New York at Binghamton.